Jainism in Early Medieval Karnataka
(c. A.D. 500-1200)

Jainism In Early Medieval Karnataka
(c. A.D. 500-1200)

RAM BHUSHAN PRASAD SINGH

Foreword by
PROF. A. L. BASHAM

MOTILAL BANARSIDASS PUBLISHERS
PRIVATE LIMITED • DELHI

Reissued: Delhi, 2008
First Edition : Delhi, 1975

ISBN: 978-81-208-3323-4

MOTILAL BANARSIDASS
41 U.A. Bungalow Road, Jawahar Nagar, Delhi 110 007
8 Mahalaxmi Chamber, 22 Bhulabnai Desai Road, Mumbai 400 026
203 Royapettah High Road, Mylapore, Chennai 600 004
236, 9th Main III Block, Jayanagar, Bangalore 560 011
Sanas Plaza, 1302 Baji Rao Road, Pune 411 002
8 Camac Street, Kolkata 700 017
Ashok Rajpath, Patna 800 004
Chowk, Varanasi 221 001

PRINTED IN INDIA

By Jainendra Prakash Jain at Shri Jainendra Press,
A-45 Naraina, Phase-I, New Delhi 110 028
and Published by Narendra Prakash Jain for
Motilal Banarsidass Publishers Private Limited,

Dedicated to
My revered Teacher
Professor Ram Sharan Sharma

CONTENTS

FOREWORD

From the time of the Mauryas Jainism was an important factor in the religious life of the area now covered by Karnataka State, formerly known as Mysore. With the support of many kings, the Jainas erected splendid temples and monasteries in many parts of the region, and the wonderful remains at Śravaṇa-Beḷgoḷa and elsewhere remain to this day as living memorials of the former greatness of Jainism, which still retains the support of many inhabitants of the area. The Jainas were pioneers in the development of the Kannaḍa language, and they contributed greatly to many aspects of the cultural life of the region.

This important factor in the development of the civilization of South India has not been adequately studied. The great majority of the scholars specialising in the subject, whether in India or elsewhere, devote most of their attention to the forms of Jainism still prevalent in Gujarat and Rajasthan, while the Digambara Jainas of the South receive much less attention, and that mainly from local scholars. I am very glad that Dr. R. B. P. Singh has helped to fill a serious gap in our library shelves by producing this excellent study, which describes the Jain religion as it existed in Karnataka in the early medieval period. He has acquired a sound knowledge of the Kannaḍa language in which many of his sources are written and with this, together with a good knowledge of Sanskrit and Prākṛit, he has produced a sound and scholarly survey of many aspects of the subject, not neglecting the social effects of Jainism on the life of the times. His work is sound, authoritative and original, and forms a very significant contribution to the study of India's religious history.

A. L. Basham

Australian National University
Canberra
28 January 1973

PREFACE

The present book has grown out of my Ph.D. thesis approved by the Patna University in 1972. It is the result of my researches into the religious history of the Jainas in Karnataka who dominated the political and cultural life of Karnataka for about one thousand years during the early medieval period. Based on an analytical study of literary and epigraphic sources, it attempts to explain the prevalence of image worship, tantrism, priesthood and ritualistic formalism which characterized Karnataka Jainism in the early medieval period. The book also seeks to examine the social and economic basis of Jaina monasteries in all parts of the Kanaḍa region.

The work has been prepared under the supervision of my respected teacher Professor R. S. Sharma, farmer Head of the Department of History, Patna University. He was not only a competent guide for my research but has also been a source of inspiration and encouragement to me. He took pains to go through the entire work in its manuscript stage and made valuable suggestions on many points. Words fail me to express my indebtedness to him.

I cannot forget Dr D. N. Jha who first kindled in me the spirit of research in south Indian history and Dr R.N. Nandi who taught me the proper way to tackle the problems of religious history. Dr Jha also read the entire revised manuscript and suggested several improvements. I am also thankful to my teachers in the Department of History, Patna University who helped me in various ways. I acknowledge with gratitude the help and advice I received from many eminent scholars from South India, especially Professor T. V. Mahalingam, Madras University, Professor P.B. Desai, Karnataka University, Dharwar, and Dr G. S. Dikshit of the same University.

I will be failing in my duty, if I do not express my deep sense of obligation to Professor A.L. Basham, who found time to go through the typescript and wrote a foreword for it. My thanks are also due to Dr. B.K. Pandeya, Dr (Mrs) Suvira Jaiswal, Jawaharlal Nehru University, Delhi, Dr. R.L. Shukla, Delhi University, Shri R.N. Kumar, Sri P.N. Sahay, Sri K.N. Rai and Sri Mahamaya Prasad of the Department of History, Patna University, Shri S. Nagaraj, Deputy librarian, The National Library, Calcutta, Shri S.P. Gunjal, Librarian, Karnataka University, Dharwar, Shri M. Surendra, Karnataka Arts College, Dharwar, and Shri Nemichandra Shastri, Librarian, Deva Kumar Oriental Jaina Library, Arrah, for their cooperation during my research.

I am also obliged to the Indian Council of Historical Research, New Delhi, for granting me a subsidy for the publication of this book, but the responsibility for the facts stated, opinions expressed or conclusions reached, is entirely mine and the ICHR accepts no responsibility for them. Mr. J.P. Jain, M/s Motilal Banarasidass, Delhi, deserves special thanks for having undertaken its publication so promptly. I pay tribute of respect to my deceased father Shri Rameshwar Prasad singh whose constant financial support enabled me to continue the research work for a fairly long period.

In spite of my best efforts, some mistakes and omissions have escaped my notice for which, I trust, my readers will kindly bear with me. They are also requested to forgive me for using both the old and new names of the present Karnataka state.

Ram Bhushan Prasad Singh

20 November 1975
B. N. College
Patna University.

SCHEME OF TRANSLITERATION

अ	a	क्	k	च्	c	ट्	ṭ	त्	t
आ	ā	ख्	kh	छ्	ch	ठ्	ṭh	थ्	th
इ	i								
ई	ī	ग्	g	ज्	j	ड्	ḍ	द्	d
उ	u	घ्	gh	झ्	jh	ढ्	ḍh	ध्	dh
ऊ	ū								
ए	e	ङ्	ṅ	ञ्	ñ	ण्	ṇ	न्	n
ऐ	ai								
औ	au								
ऋ	ṛ								
प्	p	य्	y	श्	ś	ह्	h		
फ्	ph	र्	r	ष्	ṣ	क्ष्	kṣ		
ब्	b	ल्	ḷ						
भ	bh	व्	v	स्	s	त्र	tr		
म्	m					ज्ञ्	jñ		

Anusvara ं ṁ, ñ

Visarga : ḥ

ABBREVIATIONS

ABORI	*Annals of the Bhandarkar Oriental Research Institute, Poona.*
BDCRI	*Bulletin of the Deccan College Research Institute,* Poona
BK	Book
BKI	*Bombay Karnataka Inscriptions,* Dharwar
Cf.	Compare
Ch.	Chapter
EC	*Epigraphia Carnatica,* Banglore and Manglore
Ed.	Edited
EI	*Epigraphia Indica,* Calcutta
ERE	*Encyclopaedia of Religion and Ethics,* ed. J. Hastings, Edinburgh
IA	*Indian Antiquary,* Bombay
IC	*Indian Culture,* Calcutta
IHQ	*Indian Historical Quarterly,* Calcutta
Introd.	Introduction
JA	*Jaina Antiquary,* Arrah
JBBRAS	*Journal of the Bombay Branch of the Royal Asiatic Society,* Bombay
JBU	*Journal of the Bombay University,* Bombay
JKU	*Journal of the Karnataka University,* Social Sciences, Dharwar
JSB	*Jaina Siddhānta Bhāskara,* Arrah
KI	*Karnataka Inscriptions,* Dharwar
MAR	*Mysore Archaeological Report,* Banglore
pp.	pages
pt.	part
Pro. AIOC	*Proceedings and Transactions of the All India Oriental Conference*
SBE	*Sacred Books of the East*
SBJ	*Sacred Books of the Jainas*
SII	*South Indian Inscriptions,* Madras

Top. List of *Inscriptions*	*Topographical list of Inscriptions*, *Madras*
tr.	translated
vol.	Volume
vv	Verses

ABBREVIATED NAMES OF DIFFERENT TALUQS

Ag	Arkalgud	Md	Mandya
Ak	Arsikere	Mg	Mudgere
BL	Belur	ML	Malavaḷḷi
Bn	Banglore	Mr	Malur
Ch	Chamrajnagar	My	Mysore
Cd	Citaldroog	Mj	Manjarbad
Cg	Coorg	Ng	Nagamangala
Cm	Chikmagalur	NL	Nelamangala
Cp	Cennapatna	Nr	Nagar
Dg	Davangere	SB	Sorab
Gb	Gubbi	SB	Śravaṇa-Beḷgoḷa
Gd	Goribidnur	Sh	Shimoga
Hg	Heggadadevankote	Si	Sira
Hl	Holakere	Sk	Shikarpur
Hn	Hassan	Sp	Srinivaspur
Hn	Hole-Narsipur	TL	Tirthahaḷḷi
Kd	Kadur	Tm	Tumkur
KL	Kolar	Tp	Tiptur
Kp	Koppa	Yd	Yedatore

CHAPTER I

INTRODUCTION

Karnataka or the present Mysore state stands apart as a distinct unit in the vast southern country and is situated south of Maharashtra. Its geographical boundaries are given by Wilks[1] as follows : "Commencing near the town of Bidar... following the course of Kanarese language to the south east, it is found to be limited by a waving line, which nearly touches Adoni, winds to the west of Gooty, skirts the town of Anantpur, and passing through Nandidroog, touches the range of Eastern Ghats ; thence pursuing the mountainous pass of Gazzalhati, it continues to follow the abrupt turn caused by the great chasm of western hills between the towns of Coimbtore, Pollachi and Palaghat ; and sweeping to the north-west, skirts the edges of the precipitous western Ghats, near as far north as the sources of Kṛṣṇā, whence following first an eastern and afterwards a north-eastern course, it terminates in rather an acute angle near Bidar, already described as its northern limit."

We may have some idea of the extent of Karnataka in early medieval times. The name Karṇāṭa occurs in the *Jambukhaṇḍa* of the *Mahābhārata*, the *Purāṇas* and the *Bṛhatsaṁhitā* of Varāhamihira (6th century A.D.) in the list of southern *janapadas*.[2] An epigraph of the early Kadamba King Viṣṇuvardhana I[3] indicates that the Karṇāṭa country included a group of territories and Vaijayantī or modern Banavasi in the North Kanara district of Mysore was the metropolis. The country ruled over by the early Cālukya kings of Vātāpi or modern Badami in the Bijapur district and the adjoining

1. Wilks, cited in G. Yazdani (ed.), *The Early History of the Deccan*, pts. I-VI, p. 40.
2. Ibid.
3. Ibid.

areas was known as Karnataka in the 8th century A.D.[1]

The *Kavirājamārga* or the Royal Road of Poets, which is attributed to Amoghavarṣa (A.D. 815-877), defines the extent of Karnataka as lying between the Godāvarī river in the north and the Kāverī in the south. It further states that the heart of Karnataka is the territory round Kisuvolal (Paṭṭadakal in the Bijapur district), Kopaṇa or modern Koppal in the Raichur district, Onkunda in the Belgaum district, Puligere or Lakṣameśvara in the Dharwar district.[2]

The above details suggest the inclusion of North Kanara, Dharwar, Bijapur, Raichur and Gulbarga districts of the present Mysore state within the Karnataka country in the 9th century. But it seems to be difficult to specify the exact geographical boundaries of Karnataka during the 10th-12th centuries. Some scholars have held that the original Karṇāṭa country corresponds to the Kaṇṇa-viṣaya of the Hyderabad grant of Vikramāditya I, and that it lay at the foot of Śrīśaila.[3] But there is little evidence in support of such a conjecture. The *Śaktisaṅgama Tantra*[4] defines Karṇāṭa as the country that extends from Rāmanātha to Śrīraṅga. Śrīraṅga has been placed on the banks of the Kāverī which is mentioned also in the *Kavirājamārga* as marking the southern boundary of Karṇāṭa. Śrīraṅga has been identified with the modern Serirangapatam in Mysore. As regards the identification of the place Rāmanātha, Rice held that it was an island a few miles below the junction of the Tuṅga and the Bhadra, the twin streams which united to form the Tuṅgabhadrā. There is evidence to show that part of Karṇāṭa lying to the north of the Tuṅgabhadrā was being referred to under a new name in the 12th century A.D.[5]

Fleet, after an analysis of several epigraphic records, shows that Kuntala was also included in the Kannaḍa country. It included on the south Banavasi in North-Kanara, Belgāmve and Harihar in the Shimoga district of Mysore, and Hampe

1. Wilks, cited in G. Yazdani (ed.), *The Early History of the Deccan*, pts. I-VI, p. 40.
2. Ibid. p. 41.
3. Ibid.
4. Ibid
5. Ibid. p. 42,

or Vijayanagara in the Bellary district ; to the north of these places Hāṅgal, Lakṣameśvara, Lakkuṇḍi and Gadag in the Dharwar district; farther to the north, Belgaum, Saundatti, Manolī, and Koṇṇur in the Belgaum district; and still more to the north Terdāl in the Sangali state, Bijapur itself and doubtless Kalyāṇī.[1] Kuntala had thus by the twelfth century come to denote the whole of Karṇāṭa country.

The above analysis becomes more clear from the study of the Jaina records which register gifts for the Jaina monks and monasteries in Karnataka during the 5th-12th centuries. They reveal that Karnataka comprised a greater part of the state of Mysore in the early medieval period. The present study, however, excludes South-Kanara and Bidar districts of Mysore which contain no important Jaina vestiges of the 5th-12th centuries A.D.

The Jainas constitute today a small community in Mysore, but they command great respect among the Kannaḍiga people. The reasons for this may not be quite clear unless we know something of the past history of Jainism in that area, especially the processes through which the Jainas dominated the political and cultural life of Karnataka between the 5th and the 12th century A.D.

Some work has been done on the history of Jainism in Mysore till the 5th century A.D., and something is also known about the period from *c.* A.D. 1000. But not much has been published on the period from *c.* A.D. 500 to A D. 1200, when Jainism played an important role in Mysore and in the whole of Peninsular India, Śravaṇa-Beḷgoḷa served as the epicentre of this faith.

Although Jainism made valuable contributions to the life of medieval Karnataka, it has not so far received the attention it deserves. Ayyangar, Saletore, Sharma, Deo and Desai have written the history of Jainism in the Peninsular India,[2] but

1. Wilks, cited in G. Yazdani (ed.), *The Early History of the Deccan*, pts. I-VI, p. 42.
2. Ramaswami Ayyanger and B. Seshagiri Rao, *Studies in South Indian Jainism*, Madras, 1922.
   B. A. Saletore, *Medieval Jainism*, Karnataka Publishing House, Bombay, 1938.
   S. R. Sharma, *Jainism and Karnataka Culture*, Dharwar, 1940.

even if we read all their works on the subject, we do not get an adequate and comprehensive picture of the Jaina religion in Mysore during early medieval times.

Rao, who discusses the influence of Jainism in the Andhra and Karnataka districts of the former Madras Presidency, ignores some of the main developments that characterize Jainism in Karnataka. Saletore primarily traces the development of the Jaina culture under the Vijayanagara Empire, to the comparative neglect of the earlier period. S. R. Sharma is mainly concerned with the literary and artistic achievements of the Jainas. He omits important facts regarding the Jaina system of worship and elaborate temple rituals, the monastic life and the practices of the Jaina ascetics and householders.

S. B. Deo's work also suffers from a similar weakness. He ignores the literary texts of the Digambaras who composed several important works in early medieval times. From the early centuries of the Christian era he jumps on to the 13th-14th centuries without filling up the gaps between the 5th and 10th centuries. He has tried to cover such a long period and vast area that his study of Karnataka Jainism has inevitably become disjointed and superficial.

Desai mainly concentrates on the study of Jaina inscriptions in Tamilnad and gives only a brief account of the vicissitudes of Jainism in the South. As his scope is very limited he does not take account of the Jaina literary texts, which shed welcome light on the observances of the Jainas and their philosophy in Karnataka. Thus, the available publications on Jainism do not adequately dwell upon its history in Karnataka during the 5th-12th centuries A.D.

The advent of Jainism in Mysore is assigned to the 4th century B.C. according to the Jaina tradition. It states that Bhadrabāhu and his royal disciple Candragupta Maurya migrated to the south, owing to a great famine that lasted for twelve years in the North. The two Jaina ascetics along with

---

S. B. Deo, *The History of Jaina Monachism from inscriptions and literature*, Deccan College Postgraduate Research Institute, Poona, 1956.

P. B. Desai, *Jainism in South India and Some Jaina Epigraphs*, Sholapur, 1957.

a good number of followers reached Śravaṇa-Beḷgoḷa and breathed their last on the Candragiri hill in the 4th century B.C.

No early literary and inscriptional evidence is available to support the Bhadrabāhu-Candragupta Jaina tradition. It appears first in a Śravaṇa-Beḷgoḷa epigraph of the 7th century.[1] The *Bṛhatkathākośa* of Hariṣeṇa, which was composed in *c.* A.D. 931, is the next important source of our information regarding this Jaina tradition. Narasimhachar, who has examined this tradition in great detail in his revised edition of Śravaṇa-Beḷgoḷa epigraphs, concludes that the story of Bhadrabāhu-Candragupta migration has some basis to stand.[2] But in the absence of any contemporary and corroborative evidence, it is difficult to think of the introduction of Jainism in Mysore in the 4th century B.C. The disinclination among scholars to question the veracity of the above Jaina tradition seems to have sprung from their enthusiasm to push back the antiquity of Jainism in Mysore. S. R. Sharma,[3] who has also endeavoured to prove the existence of the Jainas in Mysore during the time of Aśoka on the basis of the Kalsi Rock Edict XIII, misinterpreted the term Śramaṇa. It does not necessarily mean a Jaina monk. It might refer only to the Buddhist monk.[4] Thus, in any case till the beginning of the Christian era, we have no clear and definite evidence of the prevalence of Jainism in Karnataka.

The *Mūlācāra* of Vaṭṭakera and the *Pravacanasāra* of Kundakunda, which are roughly ascribed to the beginning of the Christian era,[5] give us some idea about the life of the Jaina monks in the South. Similarly, Sāmantabhadra who belongs to the early century of Christian era, enlightens us about the conduct of a lay novice in his *Ratnakaraṇḍa-śrāvakācāra*. We have to depend solely upon the above literary texts for the history of the early phase of Digambara monachism. Epigraphic evidence, however, is available only from the 4th century A.D. Prior to this period the history of Jainism in Karnataka has been reconstructed mainly on the basis of

1. *EC.* ii, SB. 1, p 1.
2. Ibid. Introd., p. 42.
3. S. R Sharma, *Jainism and Karnataka Culture*, p. 7.
4. B M. Barua, *Inscriptions of Aśoka*, pt. II, p. 192.
5. A. N. Upadhye, (ed.), *Pravacanasāra*, Introd., p. xxii.

traditions found in the later Jaina writings and epigraphs.

The foundation of the Gaṅga kingdom in Mysore in the second century A.D., for example, figures prominently in the Jaina tradition of the 11th-12th centuries. The Jaina teacher Siṁhanandi, who is generally credited with the creation of the Gaṅga kingdom, appears only in the later records of the Gaṅgas. We have, thus, some doubts in supporting this Jaina tradition of the creation of the Gaṅga kingdom, for, there is no mention of this event in any contemporary literary text and epigraph. It is, therefore, reasonable to assume that Siṁhanandi's account of help does not stand on solid ground. Even if we believe in this tradition, we can only presume the possibility of the relation between Siṁhanandi and the progenitor of the Gaṅga race on the ground of the events that followed one after another during the period from the 4th to the 10th centuries. From the 4th century onwards, we have ample evidence to show the close relation between the Jaina teachers and the Gaṅga kings in Mysore. The first important record dated A.D. 370[1] refers to the ācārya Vīradeva, who was the preceptor of the Gaṅga King Mādhava II. He is said to have granted some plots of land and the Kumārapura village for the benefit of the Jaina sanctuary. In another record of *c.* A.D. 425, Avinīta donated the Vennelkarni village on the advice of his preceptor Vijayakīrti.[2] These Gaṅga princes may be said to have set up the examples for the later indigenous rulers of Karnataka who continued to champion the cause of the Jaina faith in Mysore during the 5th-12th centuries. Thus, from the days of the Gaṅga rulers till the first quarter of the 12th century, Jainism prospered continuously and attained the zenith of its power and influence in Karnataka. But the conversion of the Hoysaḷa King Biṭṭideva into the religion of Rāmānujācārya in A.D. 1116 and the revival of Vīra-Śaivism under the leadership of Basava and the establishment of the Liṅgāyata faith proved detrimental to the continued prosperity of Jainism in Mysore and gave a new turn to the religious history of Karnataka. Gradually Jainism lost its grounds at the hands of the Vīra-Śaivas and Vaiṣṇava reformers.

1. *EC* x, Mr 73, pp. 172-3.
2. *EC*, x, Mr 72, pp. 171-2.

CHAPTER II

SOURCES

Nature and Importance of the Jaina Literature

Our sources are mainly literary and epigraphical. The literary texts of the Digambaras consist in the main of the narrative literature to which category belong the Jaina *Purāṇas* and epics, the didactic literary works, polemic literature and the independent philosophical treatises of eminent Jaina scholars along with their commentaries on the early texts. Literary material also includes the Jaina tāntric works, the stotra literature and the Jaina colophons. Early medieval Jaina literature is extremely rich and varied. It is noted for the creation of Jaina dogmas and ethics.

The vast Digambara literature was mainly the result of the Jaina teachings which emphasised the *śāstradāna* or the gift of the sacred knowledge including books and writing materials. Attimabbe, a pious Jaina lady of Karnataka, is said to have made a thousand copies of Ponna's *Śāntipurāṇa* at her own expense,[1] probably for distribution and for the propagation of the Jaina faith among the masses during the 10th century.

The Jaina *Purāṇas* and the epics are useful for reconstructing the history of Jainism in Karnataka. The Jainas seem to have borrowed their favourite popular themes from Brāhmaṇical and general Indian literature, which enabled them to offer to their adherents all that they could find elsewhere too. At times, they established but a very slight connection between these ancient themes and the Jaina religion; in other cases, however, they changed them to give a Jinistic appearance.[2]

Jinasena in his *Ādipurāṇa* defines a *Purāṇa* as the ancient narrative of the great personages[3] and indicates its importance for the Jainas. He observes that as these *Purāṇas* are connected

1. B.A. Saletore, *Medieval Jainism*, p. 156.
2. M. Winternitz, *A History of Indian Literature*, ii, pp. 486-7.
3. *Ādipurāṇa*, pt. I, ch. I, v. 21, p. 8.

with the lives of great men and teach the way to final liberation[1], they are also called the *mahāpurāṇa*. According to him, the *Purāṇa* should deal with eight subjects, viz, the universe, the country and its natural resources, the city and the capital, the sacred places of pilgrimage, liberality, austerities, and the four conditions of existence such as the conception of hell and heaven and the result of the meritorious and sinful acts.[2]

The Jainas also adopted popular themes from the Hindu epics and wrote works which were meant to serve their adherents as complete substitutes for the *Rāmāyaṇa* and the *Mahābhārata*.[3] The earliest of the Jaina *Purāṇas* took final shape in the composition of the Prākṛit epic *Paumacariya* of Vimala Sūri, which served as a model for all the later adaptations of the Rāma legend among the Jainas.[4]

Raviṣeṇa wrote the Sanskrit version of the Jaina *Rāmāyaṇa*, known as the *Padmapurāṇa*. The date of the *Padmapurāṇa* is explicitly mentioned in his work. He states that it was composed 1203 years after Mahāvīras's *nirvāṇa*,[5] which corresponds to A.D. 676. Repeated references to Raviṣeṇa and his work in later works such as the *Kuvalayamālā* and the *Harivaṁśapurāṇa*, reveal that he had gained a prominent place among the Jaina teachers during the 8th century A.D.

The *Harivaṁśapurāṇa*, which incorporates the story of the *Mahābhārata*, is another important Digambara text. Written by Jinasena Sūri in Sanskrit, it deals with the life of Neminātha, the 22nd Jina, and Kṛṣṇa, the 9th Nārāyaṇa or Vāsudeva of the Jaina tradition. They are depicted here as cousins. While the former renounces the world and represents the ideal for spiritual life, the latter participates in worldly affairs by taking a keen interest in the battle between Pāṇḍavas and Kauravas. The other heroes of the *Mahābhārata* are also converted into pious Jainas and are shown as adopting the life of the Jaina ascetics for attaining salvation.

In the colophon, Jinasena Sūri describes himself as a disciple of Kīrttisena, who was in turn a disciple of Amita-

1. *Ādipurāṇa*, pt. I, ch. I, v.23, p. 8.
2. Ibid ch. 4, v. 3, p. 68.
3. M. Winternitz, op. cit., p. 489.
4. Ibid. p. 493.
5. *Padmapurāṇa*, pt. III, ch. 123, v. 182, p. 425.

sena. They are said to have belonged to the Punnāḍ gaṇa.[1] He states that it was composed in the Pārśvanātha Jaina temple at Vardhamānapura in the Śaka year 705 (A.D. 783) and was completed in the Śāntinātha Jaina temple of Dostika.[2]

Vardhamānapura is still unidentified. Most scholars are inclined to agree with the view of A.N. Upadhye, who has identified it with Wadhavan in Kathiawad where Hariṣeṇa composed the *Bṛhatkathākośa* during the 10th century.[3] He further states that Punnāḍ was a provincial seat of the ancient Karnataka. The Punnāḍ Saṅgha was named after that place, for in south Indian Jainism the Saṅghas, gaṇas and gacchas were commonly named after some Jaina teacher or place. The migration of the Jaina monks from Punnāḍ to Kathiawad under the leadership of Amitasena, who is described by Jinasena Sūri as the forerunner of this Saṅgha, seems possible on account of their habit and love for touring the distant countries associated with the Jaina religion. As both Jinasena Sūri and Hariṣena glorify the Vardhamānapura in the same manner, they may have lived there.

The period from the 9th to the 12th century proved to be the most creative in the composition of the Digambara *Purāṇas* both in Sanskrit and Kannaḍa. The *Ādipurāṇa* and the *Uttarapurāṇa*, also known as the *Mahāpurāṇa* of Jinasena and Guṇabhadra, are remarkable specimens of the Jaina literature in Karnataka during the early medieval age. Upadhye rightly observes[4] that it is not only a systematic exposition of the Jaina traditional lore and principles but also an exquisite specimen of Sanskrit literature, rich in exuberant descriptions and full of poetic embellishments, both of sense and sound.

The *Mahāpurāṇa* of Jinasena and Guṇabhadra, which contains the stories of the sixty-three excellent men of the Jaina tradition, has now been generally accepted as the work

1. *Harivaṁśapurāṇa*, pt. II, ch. 66, vv. 30ff, p. 802.
2. Ibid. v, 36, p. 802.
3. A. N. Upadhye, (ed.), *Bṛhatkathākośa*, Introd., p. 121.
4. A. N. Upadhye, (ed.), *Ātmānuśāsana*, Introd., p. 9.

of the 9th century.[1] It consists of two parts, the *Ādipurāṇa* and the *Uttarapurāṇa*. The *Ādipurāṇa* has forty seven chapters and deals mainly with the life of the first Jina, Ṛṣabhadeva and his son, Bharata. Fortytwo chapters are composed by Jinasena, and the remainder is added to it by his disciple Guṇabhadra. The *Uttarapurāṇa* contains the biographies of all the remaining great figures of the Jaina tradition.

Besides the Sanskrit Jaina *Purāṇas*, several *Purāṇas* were composed in Kannaḍa. Pampa, Ponna and Ranna, who are considered to be the three gems of Kannaḍa literature, flourished in Karnataka during the 10th century. The *Ādipurāṇa* of Pampa, the *Śāntipurāṇa* of Ponna and Ajitapurāṇa of Ranna deserve special mention. They enriched the Kanarese language. Cāmuṇḍarāya, who was a general of the Gaṅga King Mārasiṁha and Rācamalla, also composed the *Cāmuṇḍarāyapurāṇa*, which contains a complete history of the twenty-four Jinas. It is the oldest extant specimen of a book, written in continuous prose and therefore enables us to gain a knowledge of the language as spoken in the 10th century A.D.[2]

In the 11th and the 12th centuries there flourished some eminent Kanarese scholars, who composed the Jaina *Purāṇas* in Kannaḍa. Among these scholars, the foremost place is assigned to Nāgacandra or Abhinave Pampa, who flourished during the reign of the Hoysaḷa King Viṣṇuvardhana. He wrote the *Mallinātha Purāṇa*, which deals with the life story of the nineteenth Jaina prophet. The work has unique value, because it preserves for us a Jaina version of the *Rāmāyaṇa* which differs in important respects from its Brāhmaṇical version.[3] Besides, we have *Neminātha Purāṇa* in Kannaḍa by Karṇapārya, which describes the story of the twenty-second Jaina prophet. It also throws light on the stories of Kṛṣṇa, the Pāṇḍavas and the Mahābhārata war. Karṇapārya flourished in Karnataka in the middle of the 12th century A.D.[4]

1. M. Winternitz, op. cit., p. 499; J. P. Jaina, *The Jaina Sources of the History of Ancient India*, p. 204; N.R. Premi *Jaina Sāhitya aur Itihāsa*, p. 140; Pannalal Jaina, (ed.), *Ādipurāṇa*, Introd. p. 20.
2. E. P. Rice, *A History of Kanarese Literature*, p. 32.
3. Ibid. p. 34.
4. Ibid. p. 36.

Though considerable portions of the Jaina *Purāṇas* are replete with legendary tales, they furnish valuable information regarding the spiritual life and religious deeds of the Jainas in Karnataka. Through these lagendary tales, the Digambaras in Karnataka always stressed the duties of the Jaina householders aspiring to attain salvation. The lives of the twenty-four Jinas, which form the main contents of the above *Purāṇas*, are held up as models for the pious Jainas. The strict observance of the principle of *ahiṁsā* or non-violence figures in most stories. The dreadful consequences of violençe and of eating the flesh form the content of the Jaina sermons.

The *Purāṇas* throw welcome light on the religious rites and practices of the Karnataka Jainas. They repeatedly refer to the observance of nudity, meditation, rain-retreat, abandonment of night's meal and taking food in a standing position. They also give us a detailed description of domestic rituals. In two chapters, the *Ādipurāṇa* explains the Jaina *saṁskāras* and their importance for the Jaina devotees. The performance of the domestic rites, which resembles the Brāhmaṇical rites, is always preceded by the worship of the Jinas in the Jaina temples.

The *Purāṇas* furnish more interesting facts about the Jaina system of worship. The *aṣṭāhnika-pūjā* or the eight-day worship, the performance of ablution and the good consequences of the Jaina adoration are extensively discussed in these Jaina *Purāṇas*. Evidence derived from these *Purāṇas* is corroborated by the epigraphs which show that the donors vied with one another in building the Jaina *basadis* and *maṭhas* and making liberal endowments for their upkeep.

The Jaina didactic literature of this period is noted for a powerful desire for righteousness. A strong sense of moral obligation, an earnest aspiration for good, a fervent and unselfish charity and generally a loftiness of aims pervade several Jain ethical works and they must have been important factors in shaping the character and ideas of the Jainas.[1] Through these ethical works, the Jaina teachers of Karnataka preached the fundamental doctrines of the Jaina religion and exposed

1. J. P. Jain, op. cit., pp. 251-2.

the weak points of other religious schools. They always tried to prove the supremacy of the Jaina faith over others by means of comparison and contrast.

The *Varāṅgacarita* of Jaṭāsiṁhanandi is the most important didactic text. It is a veritable mine of information for the conduct of the Karnataka Jainas. In this text the sage Varadatta, the chief disciple of Neminātha, the 22nd Jina, explains the meaning of Dharma (religion) at the very start. He also points out the importance of Karma-siddhānta according to which the destiny of man is determined by his own actions; the bad and the good which a man experiences in his life are the consequences of his past conduct. Thus human action is the main cause of worldly bondage.[1] For complete annihilation of this bondage, Varadatta recommends Jaina penances of twelve kinds.[2] They comprise fasting, eating less than the prescribed quantity of food, abandonment of tasteful food, the mortification of the body, meditation and so on. The prince Varāṅga is said to have become a Jaina monk by being initiated in the monastic order and attained liberation by subduing the internal and external passions and practising meditation.

As the *Varāṅgacarita* nowhere mentions the date and the name of its author, it is very difficult to determine its age. The contemporary and later writings of the Jaina scholars, however, provide some clue to the date of this text. Upadhye infers that it was composed by Jaṭāsiṁhanandi.[3] Since *Kuvalayamālā* and the *Harivaṁśapurāṇa* refer to Jaḍiya and Jaṭilamuni respectively as the authors of the *Varāṅgacarita*, he places its author at the close of the 7th century A.D.[4]

The *Yaśastilaka* of Somadeva Sūri is another important Digambara text meant for religious instructions. Written partly in prose and partly in verse, it occupies a significant position in the Sanskrit Kāvya literature. It contains long discourses on the orthodox tenets of Jainism.

1. *Varāṅgacarita*, chs. 3-4, pp. 26ff.
2. Ibid. ch. X, v. 18, p. 80
3. Ibid. Introd,, p. 10.
4. Ibid. p. 22.

Somadeva states[1] at the end of his work that he belonged to Deva saṅgha and was a disciple of Nemideva, who is said to have accepted the discipleship of Yaśodeva. He adds that he composed this work in Śaka era 881 (A.D. 959), when the Rāṣṭrakūṭa King Kṛṣṇadeva was celebrating his victories at Melpāṭi after conquering the Pāṇḍya, Coḷa, Cera, and other kings.[2] Somadeva's statement is confirmed by an epigraph of A.D. 959 found at Melpāṭi in North Arcot district.[3] Though it records the grant of a village to a Śaiva ascetic, it refers to Kṛṣṇa III's victories over the above-mentioned powers.

But this does not mean that he composed his work at the Rāṣṭrakūṭa capital Mānyakheṭa. Somadeva specifies that the work was composed at Gaṅgadhāra, which was the capital of a prince named Vagarāja, the eldest son of a Cālukyan chief Arikesari, a feudatory chief of Kṛṣṇarāja.[4] Handiqui identifies the place Gaṅgadhāra with Gaṅgawati in the Raichur district quite near the modern Dharwar in Mysore state.[5] The Prabhaṇī copper-plates,[6] which are dated in A.D. 966, also help us to determine the age of Somadeva. They record the grant of a village to Somadeva by the Cālukya chief Arikesari IV for the maintenance of the Śubhadhāma Jinālaya at modern Vemulvāda. It is therefore clear that Somadeva Sūri flourished in Karnataka during the 10th century A.D.

The *Yaśastilaka* emphasises the Jaina doctrine of non-violence. Somadeva introduces two sets of characters, Sudatta and his twin disciples Abhayaruci and Abhayamati on the one hand and the king Māridatta on the other. The former represent the ideals of Jainism, and the latter the evil spirit of violence in crude form. Māridatta, who was going to sacrifice all the living creatures including human beings at the altar of the goddess Cāṇḍamāri, is converted to the Jaina faith through the teachings of the young ascetics. The fourth chapter contains a dialogue between Yaśodhara and

1. *Yaśastilaka*, pt. ii, BK. viii, p. 419.
2. Ibid. p, 413,
3. *EI*, iv, no. 40, pp. 278ff.
4. *Yaśastilaka*, pt. ii, BK. viii, p. 419.
5. K. K. Handiqui, *Yaśastilaka and Indian Culture*, p. 4.
6. The Prabhaṇī copper-plates, cited in N. Venkataramanayya, *The Cālukyas of Vemulvāḍa*, pp. 92-4.

his mother, and shows that the son suffers badly in various rebirths because he agrees to sacrifice an effigy of a cock made out of the flour. Somadeva stresses here the motives or intentions leading to virtue or sin. The moral validity of an action, according to him, should be judged on the basis of inner feelings and not outward actions.[1]

In the last three chapters, which form an independent book called the *Upāsakādhyayana* or Readings for Laymen, Somadeva gives an exposition of the Jaina doctrines and the Jaina vows. Somadeva also defends some practices of the Jaina monks such as the practice of nudity, the custom of taking food in a standing position, and abstention from bath.[2]

Amitagati and Nayasena may be held as the successors of Somadeva Sūri in the field of composing didactic literature. Amitagati flourished in Karnataka and wrote his *Subhāṣita-ratnasaṁdoha* at the beginning of the 11th century.[3] Nayasena composed his famous work *Dharmāmṛta* during the early years of the 12th century.[4] Amitagati's work deals with the entire ethics of the Digambara Jainas, gives rules of conduct for both monks and laymen and severely criticizes the tenets of the Brāhmaṇical religion.[5] Similarly, Nayasena's *Dharmāmṛta* is a book on morals and throws light on the various forms of human virtues.

The *Puṇyāsrava-Kathākośa* of Ramachandra Mumukṣu is yet another didactic work for imparting ethical instructions to monks and laymen. It glorifies the various acts of image worship and points out the beneficial results of giving gifts to Jaina monks.[6] Though there is a great deal of controversy over the date of its composition, it has been generally assigned to a period before the middle of the 12th century A.D.[7]

1. *Yaśastilaka*, pt. ii, BK. iv, p. 136.
2 Ibid. pt. ii. BK. vi, p. 280.
3. M. Winternitz, op. cit., p. 481.
4. E. P. Rice, op. cit., p. 37.
5. M Winternitz, op. cit., p. 562.
6. A. N. Upadhye and H. L. Jain, (ed.), *The Puṇyāsrava-Kathākośa*, Introd., p. 11.
7. Ibid. p, 32.

The polemical literature of the Karnataka Jainas severely criticises the Jaina teachers and illustrates the changing character of the Jaina ascetics as well as the Jaina institutions during the early medieval age. Two of these, the *Ātmānuśāsana* of Guṇabhadra and the *Darśanasāra* of Devasena, have been fully utilized for the present thesis. The *Ātmānuśāsana*, which was composed after the demise of Jinasena in the middle of the 9th century,[1] portrays vividly the vices and demerits that overshadowed the Jaina monastic life and caused deterioration in the original standards of Jaina monks. Guṇabhadra complains of the dearth of virtuous monks[2] and he bewails that the monks have become so worldly that they succumb to sex. He compares these corrupt ascetics with the half-burnt dead body which presents an aweful sight.[3] Guṇabhadra also condemns those monks who hanker after wealth.[4] The *Darśanasāra* of Devasena, composed in the Pārśvanātha Jaina temple at Dhāra in Madhya Pradesh in the Vikram era 990 (A.D. 933)[5], attacks the false sects of the Jainas in general and indicates the disruption in the Jaina church. But the *Samayaparikṣā*, a polemical work by Brahmaśiva assigned to the first quarter of the 12th century, seeks to establish the superiority of Jainism over all other creeds.[6]

The Jaina *praśastis* or the colophons, mostly found at the end of the Jaina works, provide valuable information regarding the Jaina teachers and their spiritual lineage. They generally mention the date and the place of the composition of the literary texts, and hence form an important source for determining the age of the Karnataka Jaina teachers. Raviṣeṇa, Jinasena, Guṇabhadra and Somadeva Sūri provide such information in their respective works. Jinasena Sūri gives us the most authentic and up-to-date genealogy of the Digambara teachers who succeeded to the pontifical seat of the Puṇṇāta

1. A. N. Upadhye, (ed.), *Ātmānuśāsana*, Introd, p 10.
2. Ibid. v. 149, pp. 141-2.
3. Ibid. vv. 130-131, pp. 121-5.
4. Ibid. v.138., p.132.
5. N. R. Premi, op. cit., p. 175.
6. K. A. Nilakanta Sastri, *A History of South India*, p. 385.

Saṅgha in Karnataka. He first gives[1] the pontifical succession for the traditional 683 years after the death of Mahāvīra which ends in A.D. 156. He then starts his own genealogy which consists of 33 Jaina teachers and covers a period of 627 years. Thus we have a complete list of teachers of the Puṇṇāta gaṇa till the last quarter of the 8th century A.D.

The Jaina colophons also contain many incidental references to Jaina princes and their principalities. Guṇabhadra claims that the Rāṣṭrakūṭa king Kṛṣṇa II was his disciple.[2] On the colophon of the *Uttarapurāṇa*, Lokasena, a disciple of Guṇabhadra, praises Kṛṣṇa II and states that this work was completed in A.D. 898 at Baṅkāpura in the district of Dharwar during the rule of his feudatory chief Lokāditya.[3]

The early medieval age in Karnataka also saw the composition of numerous philosophical treatises. Of these the *Sarvārthasiddhi*, the *Paramātmaprakāśa* and the philosophical works of Nemicandra have been fully utilized for the present study. These texts expound the doctrines of the Jainas in Mysore. The Jaina view of the nature of the universe and its different attributes, which are explained as the constituent substances in Jaina philosophy, is treated in great detail in these works. They point out that the inherent characteristics of the souls, if polluted by the activities of human beings, are lost and they suffer various miseries. They also recommend the methods by which the Jainas may attain perfection. The Jaina teachers lay emphasis on the observance of the three Jewels, viz., Right knowledge, Right belief and Right conduct for the attainment of liberation.

The *Sarvārthasiddhi* of Pūjyapāda is the earliest of all the philosophical treatises, and is the most authentic commentary on the *Tattvārthasūtra* of Umāsvāmi in Sanskrit. Pūjyapāda belonged to Karnataka and was a teacher of the Nandi saṅgha, a branch of the Mūla saṅgha and Kundakundānvaya.[4] The date of Pūjyapāda has been discussed by scholars at some

1. *Harivaṁśapurāṇa*, pt. ii, ch. 66, vv. 29-31, p. 802.
2. *JBBRAS*, xii, p. 85; A. S. Altekar, *The Rāṣṭrakūṭas and their times*, p. 99.
3. *Uttarapurāṇa*, vv. 35-6, p. 577.
4. *JA*, xvi, no. 11 (December 1955), p. 51.

length. Some scholars[1] place him in the 6th-7th centuries and deny teacher-disciple relationship between Pūjyapāda and Gaṅga king Durvinīta. But the majority of modern scholars agree with the view of Rice who states that Pūjyapāda was the preceptor of Durvinīta and lived in the latter half of the 5th century and the beginning of the 6th[2].

Yogīndudeva, who has been placed in the sixth century,[3] composed the *Paramātmaprakāśa* and *Yogasāra* for expounding Jaina mysticism and philosophy. The main purpose of these works is to lay down the means by which his disciple Prabhākara Bhaṭṭa and other ambitious Jainas may gain freedom from the cycle of rebirth for ever. He effectively explains the Jaina mysticism which centres round the two concepts of *ātmā* (soul) and *paramātmā* (super spirit). He distinguishes the soul from the body[4] and points out its characteristics as eternal, uncreated, omnipresent, etc. Three divisions of the soul, viz., *bahirātmā* (external soul), *antarātmā* (internal soul), and *paramātmā* (supreme soul), resemble the divisions described in the *Samādhi-śataka* of Pūjyapāda.[5] He then points out that liberation can be obtained only through self-control.

The subject matter of the *Yogasāra* is the same as that of *Paramātmaprakāśa*. It speaks at length of the nature of the soul and its transmigratory peregrinations that plunge it into myriad of miseries in different births. He also discusses the cause of misery and freedom from it by self-realization[6] and meditating upon the soul.

Nemicandra produced works of considerable philosophical value. The *Dravya-Saṅgraha*, the *Gommaṭasāra*, and the

1. R. Narasimhachar, *MAR* (1921), p. 21; also in his address to *Pro. AIOC*, 8th session, (Mysore 1937), pp. 804-5; S. C. Shastri, *Madhyayugīnacaritrakośa*, cited in *JA*, xiii, no. 1, p. 7; E. P. Rice. op. cit., p. 26,
2. B. L. Rice, *Mysore and Coorg from Inscriptions*, pp. 35, 49, and 197; J. K, Mukhtar, *JSB*, v, no. 1.
   S. S. Sastri, *Pro. AIOC*, 8th session (Mysore 1937), 564.; B.A. Saletore, op. cit., p. 23.
3. *Paramātmaprakāśa*, Introd., p. 67.
4. Ibid. ch. i, vv. 12-4, pp. 22-3.
5. *Samādhi-Śataka*, v. 4, pp. 8-9.
6. *ABORI*, xii, pt. ii, p. 135.

Trilokasāra are attributed to him. Of these three works, the *Dravya-Saṅgraha* may be regarded as a compendium of the six substances which constitute the cosmos. There remains no doubt as to the authorship of the *Dravya-Saṅgraha* by Nemicandra, for he himself states that it was composed by Muni Nemicandra.[1] The Sanskrit commentary confirms that this treatise is a compilation of the answers given by Nemicandra to the questions put to him by *Cāmuṇḍarāya*,[2] who served the Gaṅga kings Mārasiṁha and Rācmalla IV during the last quarter of the 10th century. As *Cāmuṇḍarāya* constructed the colossal statue of Gommaṭa on the Vindhyagiri hill at Śravaṇa-Beḷgoḷa in 982[3] and is said to have been a disciple of Ajitasena and Nemicandra,[4] it seems that Nemicandra flourished during the last quarter of the 10th century.

The study of the Jaina tantric texts enables us to follow the evolution of the Jaina goddesses in Karnataka in early medieval times. They lay down the formulas and spells calculated to bestow superhuman powers on the devotees by which a person could be controlled, enmity could be caused, and an evil could be averted. Indranandi and Mallisena Sūri are primarily responsible for the systematic exposition of the occult lore in Karnataka through their treatises respectively called the *Jvālinī-kalpa* and the *Bhairava-Padmāvatīkalpa*.

The age of Indranandi, who wrote the *Jvālinīkalpa*, is evident from the verses of his own work. It was composed in the Śaka year 861 (A.D. 939) at the Rāṣtrakūṭa capital Mānyakheṭa, when the Rāṣtrakūṭa king Kṛṣṇa III was ruling there.[5] Mallisena Sūri wrote the *Bhairava-Padmāvatī-Kalpa* which consists of ten chapters and throws ample light on the tantric rites. Though Mallisena does not mention the date of the composition of his work, he clearly states that he belonged to the monastic line of the renowned teacher Ajitasena,[6] who

1. *Dravya-Saṅgraha*, v. 58, p. 123.
2. J.L. Jaini, *Gommaṭasāra Jiva-Kāṇḍa*, Introd., p. 5.
3. *EC*, ii, SB. 122, p. 50.
4. *Ibid.* Introd., p. 14.
5. *Jvālinī-Kalpa*, pp. 37-8.
6. *Bhairava-Padmāvatī-Kalpa*, ch. 10, v. 54, p. 74.

preceded the two Jaina teachers Kanakasena and Jinasena. Of these two preceptors, Jinasena was the teacher of Mallisena Sūri.[1] Ajitasena, who is repeatedly referred to in inscriptions at Śravaṇa-Belgoḷa, dated A.D. 974[2] and A.D. 995,[3] undoubtedly flourished in Karnataka during the last two decades of the 10th century. Since he is mentioned as the first teacher of the three predecessors of Mallisena Sūri, we may safely place him during the middle of the 11th century, if we assign 20 years for each generation of teachers. It is also substantiated by the statement of the author in his *Mahāpurāṇa*, wherein Mallisena states that it was composed in the Jaina temple at Mulgunda in the Gadag taluq of Dharwar district in 1047.[4]

Apart from the literary texts, contemporary inscriptions constitute our chief source for the study of the Jaina religion in Karnataka. They are full of information on the patronage of the Jaina devotees who contributed to the diffusion of culture in Karnataka in early medieval times.

The present work is based on the study of about three hundred Jaina votive and donative records. From a study of the find-spots of the Jaina records, it becomes apparent that the donative records are more numerous than the votive ones. The donative records, which register gifts of land, village, customs dues, etc. for Jaina monks and monasteries, are one hundred and seventy-five in number.[5] They are mostly in the forms of grants of land, village, garden, etc. made by the ruling class and the pious Jaina devotees of Karnataka. They are generally meant for providing necessary materials for worship, for meeting the maintenance cost of Jaina monks and monasteries, for renovation of the old *basadis*, and for running charity houses, attached to the Jaina temples.

Of the total number of inscriptions examined by us, the votive Jaina records are not more than ninety-four.[6] Out of

1. *Bhairava-Padmāvatī--Kalpa*, vv. 55-6, p. 74.
2. *EC* ii, SB. 59. p. 14.
3. Ibid. SB. 121, p 50.
4. N.R. Premi, op. cit., p. 315.
5. Cf. Districtwise arranged list of inscriptions in Appendix 'A'.
6. Cf Appendix 'B'.

these ninety-four votive records, seventy[1] have been found on Cikka-beṭṭa or Chandragiri hill at Śravaṇa-Beḷgoḷa in the Chennarayapatna taluq of the Hassan district of Mysore which has been the most important seat of Jainism from earliest times. The remaining ones belong to other parts of Karnataka.

A third type of Jaina epigraphs, which commemorate the visits to the sacred places by Jaina pilgrims, number about twenty-five.[2] They point out the importance of Śravaṇa-Beḷgoḷa for the Jainas who concentrated first in this area and gradually extended their influence in other regions of Karnataka.

Of the donative records, the Noṇamaṅgala copper plate of the 4th century may be considered a landmark in the history of Jainism in Karnataka. It is the earliest to refer to the donation of the Kumarāpura village in Malur taluq of the Kolar district to the Jaina temple at Perbbolal and provides the earliest evidence of the king's interest in Jainism in the Mysore region.

From the 5th century onwards, grants of land and village to the Jaina establishments began to increase in number, which attests to the growing influence of Jainism in several parts of Mysore. Since grants were made in favour of the Jaina teachers mainly by the kings, princes, nobles, merchants and high officials of the state, they give some idea of the social basis of Jainism in Mysore.

The donative records of our period throw light on the resources of the Jaina monasteries which emerged as landowning institutions in Mysore. They also tell us about the proliferation of the Jaina monastic orders and show how they were divided into various monastic units such as the *gaṇa*, *gaccha* and *anvaya*. Moreover, they show the extent of regional influence in the formation of Jaina saṅghas such as Navilūr, Kollaṭūr, Kittūr, etc. These saṅghas were evidently formed after

1. Cf. Appendix 'B'.
2. *EC.* ii, no. 4, 900 A.D., p. 3 ; no. 10, 800 A.D., p. 3; no. 18, 700 A.D., p. 5 ; nos. 38-4, p. 9 ; nos. 48-9, p. 10 ; nos. 410-4, pp. 80-1 ; no. 416, p. 81 ; nos. 418-9, p. 81 ; nos. 421-3, p. 82 ; no. 432, p. 83.

the names of the places which gained popularity in Karnataka during early medieval times.

Jaina epigraphs are also valuable for the study of Jaina rituals and practices. The *sallekhanā* rite or voluntary death by fasting is repeatedly referred to in the inscriptions of Śravaṇa-Beḷgoḷa. There are fifty-nine cases of such death by fasting during the 7th-8th centuries. The inscriptions not only indicate the popularity of this rite in Karnataka during the 7th-8th centuries but also its continuance in subsequent times. The available epigraphic material also shows that the Jaina laity practised *sallekhanā* as ardently as the monks and nuns.

The religious injunctions regarding the above rites in the Jaina texts are corroborated by a large number of inscriptions from Śravaṇa-Beḷgoḷa. On the basis of epigraphic references, which may be treated as behavioural data, it is possible to show how the Karnataka Jainas faithfully followed their religious principles and observed them in their day-to-day life. An epigraph of the 7th century tells us about Vṛṣabhanandi, who practised *sannyāsana* on the summit of Candragiri hill, according to the prescribed rules.[1] Māsena, another Jaina ascetic, is said to have observed the vow in the 8th century in accordance with the rules.[2] The Jaina epigraphs show that the *sallekhanā* was undertaken at the approach of death.[3] The Śravaṇa-Beḷgoḷa epigraphs also refer to the twelve types of Jaina penance.

That the temples were well established institutions in Karnataka can be inferred from large number of inscriptions which record donations for the construction and renovation of the Jaina temples. They were not merely centres of religious worship, as they are today, but rendered some useful service to the Jainas. They functioned as centres of learning and ran charity houses for the distribution of food among the Jainas. The Jaina epigraphs also throw light on the rites and practices of the Jaina worshippers who offered prayers to the Jinas in the Jaina temples. Some inscriptions indicate the exalted

1. *EC*, ii. SB. 106, p. 44.
2. Ibid. SB. 27, pp. 6-7.
3. Ibid. SB, 80, 88, 93, 99, etc.

position of the Jaina Yakṣiṇīs, who came to be worshipped in Karnataka as the most popular goddesses during the 10th-12th centuries.

The Jaina iconography is no less valuable than the Jaina epigraphs for the study of Jaina divinities in Karnataka in early medieval times. It enables us to recognize and identify the Jinas (Jaina gods), for we can spot various marks and attributes assigned to the main gods and associated deities and can determine their position in the hierarchy of Jaina pantheon. The icon bears the date and name of the sculpture which helps us fix the age and provenance of the image. Iconic representation of gods and goddesses also indicates the change, if any, in their status. The Jaina cave at Badami, for instance, shows the independent status of the Jaina Yakṣiṇīs, who previously appear to have served merely as attendant deities. Again, in the Meguti temple at Aihoḷe in the Bijapur district, the change in the position of the Jaina Yakṣiṇī Ambikā is visible. Moreover, the Jaina iconography enables us to differentiate between the southern and the northern styles of sculptures. Jaina images of south India bear the imprint of the Dravidian style.

To sum up, the study of the Jaina literary texts is essential for the knowledge of Jaina mythology and philosophy and the doctrines and rituals of the Jainas in Karnataka. The epigraphs show how far these were prevalent and how these underwent changes in early medieval times. They also give an account of the patronage extended to Jainism by kings, princes, nobles and others.

CHAPTER III

IDOL WORSHIP AND TANTRISM

In the earliest phase of their history the Jainas and the Buddhists launched a systematic campaign against the cult of ritual and sacrifice as destructive of all morals, and laid great stress on the purification of soul for the attainment of *nirvāṇa* or salvation. They denied the authority of god over human actions. Unlike the Hindus, they did not accept god as the creator and destroyer of the universe. Contrary to the popular view, they held that every soul possesses the virtues of *param-ātmā* or god and attains this status as soon as it frees itself from the worldly bondage.

Naturally the early Jainas did not practise image worship, which finds no place in the Jaina canonical literature. The early Digambara texts from Karnataka do not furnish authentic information on this point, and the description of their *mūlaguṇas* and *uttaraguṇas* meant for lay worshippers do not refer to image worship. But idol worship first appeared in the early centuries of the Christian era, and elaborate rules were developed for performing the different rituals of Jaina worship during early medieval times.

Sāmantabhadra, who belongs to the early century of the Christian era, was probably the first to lay down worship as the religious duty of a layman. He included it among the *śikṣāvratas* or educative vows and gave it a place of some importance in his rules for Jaina householders.[1] From his time, the Jaina teachers further developed their system of worship. Somadeva included it among *sāmāyika-śikṣā-vrata* or the customary worship and devoted a full chapter to the Jaina system of worship.

1. S.P. Brahmachari, *Gṛhastha-dharma*, v. 119, p. 144.

In early medieval times, the literary and epigraphic sources indicate the new outlook of Jaina teachers, who frequently recommended image worship. They thought the construction of new temples and rebuilding of old and dilapidated ones as meritorious acts. They glorified temple worship and encouraged the Jaina laity to erect *basadis*, enshrine relics in them, and visit the sacred places associated with the lives of the Jinas.

The *Paumacariya*,[1] the oldest Prākṛit kāvya, tells us about the Jaina system of worship in detail. It throws light on the worship of the Jaina images, bathing ritual of the Jinas, and installation of images.[2] The *Paramātmaprakāśa*, which is a work of the 6th century, explains that the laymen, who do not perform the worship with eight articles and do not pay reverence to the Five Perfect Beings, cannot attain salvation.[3] It is apparent that the worship of the Jina became a necessary condition for the attainment of liberation. The *Padmapurāṇa*, composed by Ravisena in the 7th century A.D., exhorts the people to perform Jina worship and erect Jina images for the attainment of temporal as well as eternal blessings.[4] It also ordains the Jaina devotees to make arrangements for flower, incense, and light in Jaina temples. It further lays down that a man can accomplish the most difficult worldly task by performing Jina worship and installing images of Jinendra.[5]

The *abhiṣeka* or the bathing ritual of the Jinas, which is held in high esteem among the Karnataka Jainas, is also referred to in the Jaina texts. The most detailed description of this rite[6] is furnished by Jaṭāsiṁhanandi who wrote the *Varāṅgacarita* in the 7th century. The text draws attention to the merits of building temples, setting up images and conducting Jina

1. The date of *Paumacariya*, composed by Vimalasūri is very controversial. According to some scholars it was written in the 1st century A.D.; according to others, led by Jacobi, it was composed in the 3rd century A.D. The view of Jacobi has been generally accepted by scholars.
2. M. Santilal Vora. (tr.), *Paumacariya*, pt. i, ch. 32, v. 70ff., p. 252ff.
3. A N. Upadhye, (ed.), *Paramātmaprakāśa*, v. 168, p. 312.
4. *Padmapurāṇa*, pt. i, ch. 14, vv. 92-3, p. 313.
5. Ibid. v. 213, p. 321.
6. *Varāṅgacarita*, ch. 23, v. 60ff, pp. 225-6.

worship. It repeats the idea that a layman who is always engaged in worldly pursuits must worship the Jina for his final liberation from the cycle of births and deaths.[1] It also speaks of the morning and evening worship of the Jinas in Jaina temples.

Besides the above Jaina texts, the *Yaśastilaka* of Somadeva Sūri and the *Vasunandi-Śrāvakācāra* contain much information regarding the image worship. Vasunandi for instance speaks of the good results of performing the eight-fold worship of the Jinas. The devotees are said to have attained both the temporal as well as eternal happiness in the present life and in the life after death.[2] The offerings of unboiled rice, flower, sweets, umbrella, etc, to the Jinas are said to have led to good physical health, victory over enemies on the battlefield and attainment of eternal blessings.[3]

Literary evidence regarding Jaina image worship is corroborated by contemporary inscriptions which record grants of land and village to Jaina establishments and to Jaina monks for erecting temples, repairing them and performing worship. The Kadamba records inform us that the worship of the Jina was the most favourite way of expressing Jaina devotion. They show that the Kadamba kings faithfully followed the sacred injunction of the Jaina teachers with regard to the image worship. They made lavish donations to Jaina temples, and erected new temples in the north-western parts of Mysore. In order to make the worship effective in public life, the Kadamba king Ravivarmā, issued an ordinance that the festival of Jinendra lasting for eight days should be celebrated regularly every year on the full moon of the month of Kārttika or November from the revenues of the village Purukheṭaka ; that the worship of Jinendra should be perpetually performed by the pious countrymen and citizens.[4] In view of this record it is not surprising that the Kadamba king not only performed Jina worship him-

1. *Varāṅgacarita*, ch. 22, v. 33 ff, pp. 215-6.
2. Hiralal Jain, (ed.), *Vasunandi-Śrāvakācāra*, v. 493, p. 136.
3. Ibid. vv. 483-92, pp. 135-6.
4. *IA*, vi, no. 22, p. 27.

self but also imposed it on the people.

The people of Karnataka followed their kings in matters relating to image worship. They paid reverence to Jinas by constructing Jaina temples, and making proper arrangements for the repairs and maintenance of the same. An epigraph, belonging to the reign of the Cālukya king Kīrtivarman II, which is dated in the 6th year of his reign, commemorates the construction of a Jaina temple by Kaliyamma, the gāvuṇḍa of Jebulageri in the district of Dharwar.[1] Another record registers a gift of 500 *nivartanas* of land for the worship and offerings to the god Śaṅkha Jinendra by Durgāśakti of the Sendraka family during the reign of Pulakeśin II.[2] Similar other epigraphs speak of the donation of land to the god Śaṅkha-Jinendra at Lakṣmeśvar in the district of Dharwar during the 7th-8th centuries.

Similar evidence may be adduced to show the prevalence of image worship during the time of the Rāṣṭrakūṭas. The Koṇṇur inscription of the Rāṣṭrakūṭa king Amoghavarṣa furnishes evidence of the Jaina devotion of Bankeya, the feudatory chief, who is said to have founded a Jaina temple at Koḷanūr or Koṇṇur in the district of Dharwar and granted land in the village Taleyūr for the benefit of that temple during the 9th century.[3] Another record describes a vaiśya named Cīkārya as erecting a Jaina temple at Mulgund in the same district during the rule of the Rāṣṭrakūṭa king Kṛṣṇa II in the 10th century.

In the 11th-12th centuries, the Jaina teachers from Karnataka made equally zealous effort for propagating the idea of image worship among the Jainas who responded to their appeal by erecting many new *basadis* in different parts of Mysore. This is substantiated by the donative records of the later western Cālukyas, the Hoysaḷas, the Śāntaras and their feudatory chiefs,[4] who made liberal gifts of lands and villages for the continuous performance of Jina worship. They also

1. *BKI*, i, pt. i, no. 5, p. 3.
2. Ibid. iv, no. 3, p. 2.
3 *EI*, vi, no. 4, p. 34.
4. Cf. Districtwise arranged list of Inscriptions in Appendix—"A".

gave impetus to this practice by renovating some of the old Jaina temples aud renewing the old charters of gifts for promoting the cause of Jina worship in Karnataka. From a record of 1068,[1] a Jaina general of the western Cālukya king Someśvara II, succeeded in converting a wooden temple into a stone structure. For this meritorious work, he took the help of the king as well as his provincial ruler Lakṣmaṇa who completely remodeled the Jaina temple at Balipura in the Vanavāsī country and endowed land to it. In A.D. 1072,[2] the queen of Someśvara II is recorded to have renewed the endowment of the village Gudigere for the Ānesejjeya *basadi*, which had been built by Kuṁkumamahādevī, the younger sister of the Cālukya king Vijayāditya. In another record of Śravaṇa-Beḷgoḷa dated A.D. 1118[3] Gaṅga-Rāja, who is praised for his meritorious work, renovated and restored all the *basadıs* in Gaṅgavāḍi. In a later record, which is dated A.D. 1184,[4] it is stated that the Gaṅgavāḍi 96,000 province shone like Kopaṇa through the efforts made by Gaṅga-Rāja. We have similar account of the religious deeds of Huḷḷa who delighted in restoring Jina temples and performing Jina worship therein. He renovated a Jaina temple at Baṅkāpura which had gone to complete ruin.[5]

Besides the worship of Jinas, there is epigraphic evidence[6] to show the regular performance of the worship of Gommaṭeśvara on the Vindhyagiri hill at Śravaṇa-Beḷgoḷa. Gommaṭeśvara was the son of the first Jina Ādinātha whose image was consecrated first by Cāmuṇḍarāya in the 10th century. He came to occupy an important position in the hierarchy of Jaina gods and his worship developed as an independent cult in Mysore in the 11th-12th centuries.

It is clear from the above-cited epigraphic references that image worship tended to continue among the Jainas of

1. *EC*, vii, sk. 135. pp. 102-4.
2. *BKI*, iv, no. 46, p. 51.
3. *EC*, ii, SB 73, pp. 38-40.
4. Ibid. iv, Ng. 32, p. 120.
5. Ibid. ii, SB 345, pp. 147-9.
6. Ibid. SB 237-8, A.D. 1196-8, p. 101 ; SB 241 ; A.D. 1175, p. 103 ; SB 242, A.D. 1175, pp. 103-4 ; SB 256, A D. 1181, p. 115.

Karnataka during the period under study. It became popular not only with royal families but also with nobles, generals, merchants and the people of different professions. But it is to be borne in mind here that this practice of Jina worship was spread and strengthened in Karnataka through royal efforts. Its gradual progress among the masses may be traced from the higher strata to the lower level of the Karnataka society.

The reasons which impelled the Jaina teachers of Karnataka to encourage the laity to perform image worship are not difficult to find out. The practical idea of gaining popularity among the people and removing the Brāhmaṇical hatred against the Jainas made frequent provisions for the adoration of icon-worship. In order to compete with the Brāhmaṇas, it was felt necessary to rid Jainism of the dry asceticism. The economic considerations of the Jaina teachers also prompted them to propagate this practice. Through their advocacy of image worship, they acquired new means of livelihood in Jaina monasteries and temples, which were invariably endowed with rich gifts of land, village and customs dues in the early medieval period.

Jaina Motive of Worship

It is generally held that the worship of the Jinas is undertaken for spiritual reasons and not for gaining any worldly benefit. Professor A.N. Upadhye observes[1] that the aspirants (the Jaina worshippers) receive no boons, no favours and no cures from him by way of gifts from the divinity. As the Jina is the embodiment of perfection, the Jaina worshippers pray to him, worship him and meditate on him as a model that they too might become perfect. Another scholar states[2] that the Jainas ask for nothing from the Jinas; nor are they supposed to be granting boons to their devotees. They are not worshipped because worship is pleasing to them but because it is the source of the greatest good—the attainment of godly perfection for our soul. Kalaghatgi,[3] declares that

1. A.N. Upadhye (ed.), op. cit., Introd.. p. 36.
2. C.R. Jain, *Essays and Address*, p. 126.
3. T.G. Kalaghatgi. *JKU*, iii, p. 18.

for a Jaina it is not necessary to surrender to any higher being nor to ask for divine favour. There is no place for divine grace nor for the whims of a superior deity for the sake of attaining liberation. Stevenson[1] too supports the same view. She holds that the attitude of Jaina worshipper seems nearer to the French soldier paying homage at the tomb of Napoleon and saluting the memory of a great hero than to the warm personal adoration and loving faith connected with the Hindu idea of *bhakti*. All this would suggest that the devotees offered obeisance to the Jinas for realizing the virtues of the Jinas in their own lives and not for any worldly gain.

But it is difficult to accept the views expressed above. The Jainas performed worship not out of selfless devotion but from a desire to gain temporal as well as eternal blessings and happiness. Like the Hindus, the Jainas completely surrendered to the Jinas and expected favour from them. It is also wrong to think that the Jinas did not dispense divine grace to their devotees. The Jaina *Purāṇas* and the stotra literature of the Karnataka Jainas reveal the fact that the Jainas were moved by the same feelings and desires as are found in any ordinary human being. They appeal to the Jinas as ardently as the Hindus to Brahmā and Viṣṇu. From the study of the *Bhaktāmara stotra* of Mānatuṅga, it is apparent that the devotee can get victory over the enemies[2] and escape the grip of disease[3] by remembering the name of the first Jina Ādinātha. Mānatuṅga himself is said to have released himself from the bondage of forty-two chains by the mere recitation of the name of the Jina.[4] The *Harivaṁśapurāṇa* of Jinasena Sūri also repeats the same idea and states that one can release himself from the influence of evil spirits by uttering the name of the Jina.[5]

The *Varāṅgacarita* refers to the various results of performing Jina worship with eight different articles. Each article of

1. S. Stevenson, *ERE*, x, p. 188.
2. N.R. Premi, tr., *Ādināth-Stotra*, v. 43, p. 47.
3. Ibid. v. 45, p. 50.
4. I id. v. 46, p. 51.
5. *Harivaṁśapurāṇa*, pt. ii, ch. 66, v. 41, p. 804.

offering is supposed to confer on the devotees a different boon. Thus the offering of unbroken rice results in long life[1] and that of curd leads to the accomplishment of the desired work.[2] The worship of the Jinas is said to have resulted in the attainment of the desired things.[3] Jinasena and Guṇabhadra, who composed the *Mahāpurāṇa* in the 9th century, also describe the Jinas as those who grant the desired results to the laymen.[4] A man who wants wealth and prosperity should concentrate his mind on the Jainas who are described as the giver of the heaven.[5] The devotee can rid himself of the disease and bondage and can free himself from the clutches of lion, snake and fire.[6] King Bharata is said to have marched against his enemies in the south direction after offering worship to the Jina.[7] The importance of Jina worship with eight different articles is also repeated by Vasunandi,[8] who composed the *Vasunandi-Śrāvakācāra* in the early years of the 12th century.[9]

The Karnataka Jaina teachers always glorified and attributed divine grace to the Jinas. They devoted their talents to the deification of Mahāvīra and other Jinas. The Jinas, who had been earlier regarded as simply spiritual teachers revealing the truth and inspiring the followers of Jainism in attaining liberation (*mokṣa*), came to be regarded as gods among the Jainas in Karnataka in the early medieval period. Thus, the Jinas were credited with the same attributes of divinity as characterized the Brāhmaṇical gods Śiva, Viṣṇu and Brahmā. Analogy between the Jinas and the Hindu divinities continued to persist among the Jainas as late as the 13th century. Āśādhara, who composed the *Jinasahasranāma* in the middle of the 13th century,[10] attributes one thousand and eight names to the

1. *Varāṅgacarita*, ch. 23, v. 20, p. 222.
2. Ibid. v. 19, p. 222.
3. Ibid., ch. 22, v. 46, p. 216.
4. *Ādipurāṇa*, pt. 1, ch. 7, v. 281, p. 163.
5. Ibid. v. 265, p. 165.
6. Ibid. v. 303, p. 165.
7. Ibid. pt. ii, ch. 29, v. 1, p. 62.
8. H.L. Jain, (ed.), *Vasunandi-Śrāvakācāra*, Introd. p. 19.
9. Ibid. vv. 483-93. pp. 135-6.
10. H.L. Jain. (ed.), *Jinasahasranāma*, Introd. pp. 22-3.

Jina and indicates the significance of uttering them correctly.[1] The Jina is repeatedly compared with Mahādeva,[2] Sadāśiva[3] and Brahmā[4]

The exaltation of the position of the Jinas is well illustrated in the prayer hymns addressed to them in the Jaina *Purāṇas*. Ravisena, who flourished in the 7th century, identifies the first Jina Ādinātha with the Hindu gods Śiva and Svayambhū.[5] Like his predecessor, Jinasena too describes the Jina as Brahmā, Viṣṇu and Svayambhū.[6] Almost all the epithets and names, expressive of his qualities, functions and associations are liberally ascribed to the Jinas with some explanation. Ṛiṣabhadeva is again compared with Śaṁkara and other Hindu gods.[7]

Although in the early days, the Jainas criticised the Hindu theory of creation and destruction, in later times the Jinas are assigned both the creative and destructive power. In the *Mahāpurāṇa* of Jinasena-Guṇabhadra, the Jina is spoken of as the creator[8] and destroyer[9] of the universe. Literary evidence is also supported by a 10th century epigraph which refers to the Jina or Jinapati, adored by the gods as the First Creator of the world.[10]

The Jinas, who were represented previously as ideal personalities, were also credited with all the divine qualities of the Brāhmaṇical deities such as Brahmā and Kṛṣṇa. The Jaina teachers accepted several strange incarnations of Ṛṣabhadeva. Jinasena explains the ten incarnations of the First Jina,[11] and tries to prove that he represents Kṛṣṇa and Viṣṇu.

1. H.L. Jain. (ed.), *Jinasahasranāma*, vv. 140-3, p. 140.
2. Ibid. v. 63, p. 86.
3. Ibid. v. 104, p. 113.
4. Ibid. v. 98, p. 108.
5. *Padmapurāṇa*, pt iii, ch. 98, vv. 66-7, p. 221.
6. *Ādipurāṇa*, pt i, ch. 24, vv. 34-6, p. 576.
7. Ibid. ch. 25, v. 74, p. 601.
8. Ibid. ch. 24, v. 55, p. 578.
9. Ibid. v. 44, p. 577.
10. S.R. Sharma, op. cit. p. 143.
11. *Ādipurāṇa*, pt. i, ch. 14, v. 51, p. 309

It appears reasonable to assume that the Jaina mythologists could not keep themselves free from the influence of the Hindu conception of the creative power of gods. Thus, the Jinas were given Hindu orientation in order to adjust Jainism to changing times and as such the people were attracted towards the beneficial power of the Jaina divinities.

Jaina Objects of Worship

The Karnataka Jaina literature and epigraphs indicate that the Jaina objects of adoration resemble mainly the Brāhmaṇical objects of worship. Like the Hindus, the Jainas show their reverence not only to the Jinas alone but also to their associated deities, sacred things and symbols. The attendant deities of the Jinas and their emblems are also shown great reverence.

The Jaina objects of worship may be enumerated under the following heads ; (i) the Five Exalted Beings ; (ii) the attendant deities of the Jinas ; (iii) symbolical objects of worship ; and (iv) worship of the sacred places. Besides, the Jainas also imitated the Hindu practice of paying homage to the family members of the Jinas.

The Jainas first adore the Five Exalted Beings (the *pañcaparameṣṭhī*). They are, according to Somadeva,[1] the *arhat*, that is, one of the Jinas endowed with superhuman qualities ; the *siddha* or one who has realised within himself the luminous presence of the Infinite soul ; the *Ācārya* or the teacher who regulates the social order according to the principles of Jainism ; the *upādhyāya* or the preceptor who has mastered the sacred lore ; and the *sādhu* or the ordinary monk bent on salvation and engaged in rigorous austerities in the face of insuperable obstacles. They are thus a group of five graded purified souls. While the former two have freed themselves from the cycle of births and deaths, the remaining three are on the way of attaining salvation. Just as there are ranks in society so also there are ranks in the Jaina religious organization.

1. K.K. Handiqui, op. cit. pp. 269-70.

The worship of these exalted souls prominently figured in the devotional Jaina literature. It was prevalent among both the monks and the laymen. As the monks did not use idols, they offered only mental salutation to them in course of practising austerities.

In the temple worship, which was especially meant for ordinary men, the Jinas were assigned the foremost place among the purified souls because they are believed to reveal the path of salvation to the mankind. While the devotees performed the various acts of Jaina worship, they offered salutation to them along with the Jinas.

The Jainas of Karnataka promulgated a formula to be recited at the time of worship. This was considered to be very important in the Jaina system of adoration, and may be compared with the *gāyatrī mantra* of the Vedic school. It consists of thirty-five letters,[1] and several methods of uttering it are prescribed. Jinasena in his *Ādipurāṇa* refers to the recitation of sixteen, eight, six and five letters of the Jaina formula.[2] Sometimes it is to be limited to a single letter formula such as "Om". Somadeva too refers to the different methods of uttering the Jaina formula, but the one consisting of thirty-five letters is held to be most authoritative by him.[3]

The Jaina literature and epigraphs also refer to the worship of the attendant gods and goddesses of the Jinas (yakṣas and yakṣiṇīs). They are depicted on the right and the left sides of the Jinas in the Jaina sculpture and are recognized by their respective features. Among the numerous deities, the cult of Padmāvatī and Jvālāmālinī gained wide popularity among the Jainas in Karnataka. Independent tantric Jaina texts such as the *Bhairava-Padmāvatī-Kalpa* and the *Jvālinī-Kalpa* indicate the increasing importance of these two goddesses in Karnataka during the early medieval age. The two texts show that they were worshipped as independent tantric deities possessing mystical powers during the 11th-12th centuries.

1. K.K. Handiqui, op. cit. p. 272.
2. *Ādipurāṇa*, pt. i, ch. 21, v. 231 ff, p. 499.
3. K.K. Handiqui, op. cit. p. 272.

The Brāhmaṇical practice of worshipping religious and spiritual symbols also influenced Jainism in Karnataka. Literary evidence speaks of the worship of the following symbols; (1) *dharmacakras* or the wheels of righteousness ; (ii) the *caitya* tree, (iii) Jina-flags containing the figures of elephant, lion, peacock, bull, etc., (iv) the *mānastambha* or standing pillar. All these symbols stand for the Jinas, and they are revered, if not worshipped independently by the Karnataka Jainas. Jinasena in his *Ādipurāṇa* refers to their worship. He informs us that the Jaina tomb contained the image of the Jinas, and the people felt happy in worshipping them.[1] The worship of the *caitya* trees,[2] the wheels of righteousness, Jina-flags[3] and *mānastambha*[4] are also referred to in the same text.

The footprints of the Jaina teachers were also venerated by the Jainas in Karnataka. The *Jaina Purāṇas* enjoin the laymen to bow down at the feet of spiritual teachers. It was regarded as a pious act for the laity. As a natural consequence, the devotees felt the necessity to pay homage to those spiritual teachers even after their deaths. They began to engrave for personal adoration the foot-prints of Jaina teachers on stone or some lasting material. It became gradually a popular practice among the Karnataka Jainas.

Literary reference is also corroborated by epigraphs. An epigraph[5] of the 10th century states that the foot-marks of the teacher, Jaṭāsiṁhanandi, were carved out by Cāvaya. As Jaṭāsiṁhanandi flourished during the 7th century, his foot-prints were engraved by the devotee for personal worship in the 10th century. Cāmuṇḍarāya is also said to have paid homage to the foot-prints of Bhadrabāhu.[6] The worship of the same teacher is again referred to in another Śravaṇa-Beḷgoḷa epigraph.[7] It states that Jinacandra bows to the feet

1. *Ādipurāṇa*, pt. i, ch. 22, v. 269, p. 533.
2. Ibid. pt. ii, ch. 33, v. 86, p. 138.
3. Ibid. vv. 93-5, p. 139.
4. Ibid. v. 75. p. 137.
5. P.B. Desai, op. cit. Inscription no. 20, p. 344.
6. *EC*, ii, Introd. p. 13.
7. Ibid. SB 166, p. 79.

of Bhadrabāhusvāmī. There are clear indications of the repetition of the practice of paying reverence to the Jaina teachers in more than five Śravaṇa-Beḷgoḷa epigraphs[1] which belong to the 12th century.

The spiritual hierarchy of the Brāhmaṇical Gods influenced the Jaina pantheon in Karnataka, and the Jainas paid reverence not only to the Jinas but also to members of their family. If the sons of Śiva (Kārttika & Gaṇeśa) are worshipped in the Hindu religion, son of the first Jina Ādinātha is equally preferred for worship in the Jaina religion. In a Śravaṇa-Beḷgoḷa epigraph of the 10th century, it is stated that Cāmuṇḍarāya caused to be made the statue of Gommaṭa and he is said to have consecrated this image.[2] The worship of Gommaṭeśvara gained wide popularity among the Jainas of Karnataka by the end of the 12th century. In A.D. 1159,[3] the Hoysaḷa King Narasimhadeva gave gift of the village Savaneru for the eight-fold worship of the same image. There are similar other inscriptions from Śravaṇa-Beḷgoḷa, dated in A.D. 1175,[4] A.D. 1181[5] and A.D. 1196,[6] which contain information about the public adoration of Gommaṭeśvara on the Vindhyagiri hill and register gifts of land for providing flowers and other materials for worship. The above instances leave no doubt that the son of the first Jina came to be worshipped among the Jainas as an independent god by the end of the 12th century.

The worship of the sacred places (*nirvāṇakṣetra*) was also an object of Jaina adoration. The Jainas of Karnataka paid respect to the places which were connected with the lives and attainment of liberation of Jinas and other eminent Jaina teachers. Several epigraphs from Śravaṇa-Beḷgoḷa prove this.[7]

1. *EC*, ii, SB 119, A.D. 1100, p. 49 ; SB 123, A.D. 1100 ; SB 124, A.D. 1100, p. 50 ; SB 428, A.D. 1100, p. 82.
2. Ibid. SB 175-6, p. 89.
3. Ibid. SB 349, pp. 151-4.
4. Ibid. SB 240-2, pp. 101-4.
5. Ibid, SB 256, p. 115.
6. Ibid. SB 237, p. 101.
7. Ibid. SB 10, A.D. 800, p. 3 ; SB 4, A.D. 900, p. 3 ; SB 38-9, A.D. 750 and A.D. 950, p. 9 ; SB 40, A.D. 990, p. 9 ; SB 41-2 ; A.D. 1000, p. 9; SB 43, 44, 48, A.D. 1100, pp. 9-10; SB 410, 413, 417, A D. 1000, pp. 80-1.

The *Vasunandi-Śrāvakācāra* also corroborates the above Jaina practice.[1]

Forms of Jaina Worship

The Jaina texts of Karnataka generally refer to two forms of image worship, (1) the *bhāva-pūjā* or the mental offering of prayer to the Jinas and (2) the *dravya-pūjā* or the eight-fold worship of Jina images. The *Varāṅgacarita*[2] clearly refers to them and points out the difference between the two forms. The *bhāva-pūjā* means concentration of mind on the various qualities of the chosen deities, i.e. the Jinas. The *dravya-pūjā* denotes the proper worship of the Jina image with elaborate rituals and offering of eight different articles such as unboiled rice, sandal, incense, water, fruit, flower, etc., to the Jinas. As the *bhāva-pūjā* is performed with or without the use of idols, it is prevalent both among the Jaina monks and laymen. If the Jina image is not available, Somadeva[3] advises the Jainas to visualize the picture of the Jina on a piece of birch bark or cloth or wooden board or a slab of stone or on sand or in the air or in one's heart.

In the *Ādipurāṇa* Jinasena subdivides the *dravya-pūjā* into four categories, of which we have first the *sadārcana-pūjā* or daily worship of the Jinas.[4] The devotees daily offer sandal, unbroken rice, incense, fruit, flower and sweets to the Jinas in the Jaina temples. The erection and installation of the images and donation of villages, lands and fields fall under this category. The second form of worship is known as *caturmukha-pūjā*,[5] in which the devotee worships the four faces of the Jina. The third form is known as the *cakravartī-pūjā*, in which the royal devotee makes lavish charities according to the desires of almsmen after the performance of Jina worship.[6] Lastly comes the *aṣṭāhnika-pūjā* or the eightfold worship, which lasts for eight days. Jinasena prescribes it for all the pious countrymen.[7]

1. H.L. Jain. (ed.), *Vasunandi-Śrāvakācāra*, v. 452, p.130.
2. *Varāṅgacarita*, ch. 22, v. 43 ff, p. 216.
3. *Yaśastilaka*, ii, p. 373, cited in K.K. Handiqui, op. cit. p. 269.
4. *Ādipurāṇa*, pt. ii, ch. 38, vv. 27-8, p. 242.
5. Ibid. v. 30, p. 242.
6. Ibid. v. 31, p. 242.
7. Ibid. v. 32, p. 242.

Professor Robert Williams[1] strongly criticises this classification as unreal but does not give any grounds for this. Jinasena's classification reflects the needs of different social classes in Karnataka. He seems to have chalked out a plan for worship based on economic considerations.

Jaina Temple Worship

The prevalence of icon worship among the Jainas in Karnataka indicates the existence of the institution of temples, which are commonly known as the *basadi* or *basti* in Karnataka. Both the epigraphic and literary sources speak of the erection of Jaina temples and consecration of Jina images in the early medieval age.

The Karnataka Jainas believed that temple building was also a means to salvation and secured for the builder the delights of heaven in the next life. This accelerated the process of temple construction and gradually gave rise to several temple cities in Karnataka. Śravaṇa-Beḷgoḷa, Halsi, Aihoḷe, and Dharwar are fine witnesses to this spirit of Jaina devotion.

The people attached great importance to temple worship. They performed almost all sacraments such as birth ceremony, investiture of the sacred thread, and marriage before the Jinas in Jaina temples. Jinasena explains clearly the observation of these rites in the Jaina temples.[2]

The *Jaina Purāṇas* inform us that the votaries showed their devotion to the Jaina temple by going round the temple; this was called the circumambulation rite. The Jaina devotees are advised to perform this ritual as soon as they enter the temple.

Temple worship was both public and private. Public worship comprised the Jaina practice of daily worship of the Jina image and periodical worship on special occasions. Numerous inscriptional evidences, dating from the 5th to the 12th centuries, speak of public temple worship among the Karnataka Jainas. The earliest indication of the congre-

1. Robert Williams, *Jaina Yoga*, p. 216.
2. *Ādipurāṇa*, pt. ii, ch. 38, v. 69ff, pp. 245 ff.

gational worship is furnished by the Kadamba copper plates, which are assigned to the middle of the 5th and the 6th centuries. In one of these copper plates, it is stated that the Kadamba king Ravivarmā in his 34th regnal year granted land in Asuṇḍi in the district of Dharwar for performing worship of the Jinas.[1] Another record[2] of the same monarch refers to the performance of the eightdays worship of the Jinas by the pious Jaina devotees at Palāśika or modern Halsi in the district of Belgaum. It shows that the common people participated in the performance of the Jina worship. Harivarmā, another king of the Kadamba lineage, is also said to have granted the village Vasantavāṭaka for providing annually at the eightday's sacrifice and the perpetual anointing of the Jina image with clarified butter for the temple of the *Arhat* (Jina) which Mṛigeśavarmā had caused to be built at modern Halsi in the district of Belgaum.[3] The stone mansion of Jinendra was erected at Aihoḷe by Ravikīrti, who had obtained the favour of the Cālukya king Pulakeśin II in the 7th century.[4] Ladies of upper classes showed equal enthusiasm for public worship by erecting Jaina temples in Mysore. An epigraph of the 8th century informs us that Kaṇḍācī, the wife of a feudatory chief, constructed an auspicious Jaina temple named Lokatilaka-Jinālaya for promoting Jina worship.

Inscriptions also attest the practice of temple construction during the 9th and the 10th centuries. Cāmuṇḍarāya, the minister and general of the Gaṅga king Mārasiṁha, is said to have constructed a magnificent temple, containing the image of the twenty-second Jina Neminātha on the Vindhyagiri hill at Śravaṇa-Beḷgoḷa.[5] The upper storey of the temple was added by the son of Cāmuṇḍarāya, and an image of the twenty-third Jina Pārśvanātha was placed in it.[6] Both these temples were built in the 10th century.

1. *MAR*, 1933, no. 1, pp. 113-4.
2. *IA*, vi, no. 22, p. 27.
3. Ibid. vi, no 25, p. 31.
4. *EI*, vi, no. 1, pp. 11-2.
5. *EC*, ii, Introd p. 6.
6. Ibid.

Construction of temples and installation of Jina images therein increased in the 11th-12th centuries. Epigraphic evidence shows that princes[1] and people[2] alike erected numerous Jaina temples and granted land for various acts of worship in Jaina temples, which were open to all irrespective of caste and creed. The Jaina women of Karnataka expressed their deep devotion for Jainism by erecting a number of new *basadis* and endowing them with rich gifts. In 1047, Akkadevī is said to have granted land for meeting the cost of plastering the broken monastery of the Goṇaḍa-Beḍaṅgi Jinālaya at Vikramapura in the Bijapur district and for the supply of scent, incense and lamp.[3] Another woman, who figures prominently in the record of the 12th century, was Pocikabbe,[4] the mother of Gaṅga-Rāja. She is said to have erected numerous Jaina temples at Śravaṇa-Beḷgoḷa and many other holy places. In 1123 Śāntaladevī, the queen of the Hoysaḷa king Viṣṇuvardhana, built the Savatigandhavārṇa temple at Beḷgoḷa and granted the village Moṭṭenavile to her preceptor for providing regular worship.[5] In a record of the last quarter of the 12th century, Haryyale, a woman belonging to the middle class of Karnataka society, is said to have advised her son to build Jaina temple for obtaining boundless merit.[6] The above examples show clearly what interest both the kings and their subjects took in building Jaina temples in Karnataka during the 11th-12th centuries.

Commenting upon the prevalent modes of Jaina worship, Professor Bhattacharya observes[7] that the Jainas in optional cases keep an image in their houses and do not undergo the

1. *EC*, vii, Sk. 136, A.D. 1068, p. 103 ; *MAR*, 1927 A D. 1062, p. 43 ; *EC*, iv, Ag. 99, A.D. 1079, p. 263 ; *EC*, viii, Ng. 40, A D. 1087, pp. 144-5 ; *EC*, v, Cn 148, A.D. 1094, p. 190 ; *EC*, iv, Ng. 19, A.D. 1118, p. 116.
2. *EI*, xvi, A.D. 1053, p. 57 ; *EC*, vii, SK. 124, A.D. 1077, p. 96 ; *EC*, vi, Cm. 160, A.D. 1103, p. 57 ; *MAR*, 1939, p. 194 ; *EC*. iv, Ng, A.D. 1142, p. 138.
3. *EI*, xvii, p. 123.
4. *EC*, ii, SB 118, p. 48-9.
5. Ibid. SB 132, p. 60
6. *EC*, xii, TP. 93, p. 60
7. B C. Bhattacharya, *Jaina Iconography*, p. 21.

special ritualistic formalism in their private worship. But it seems to be difficult to subscribe to his view. Although epigraphic sources are silent on this point, several literary texts of the Digambaras contain instructions for installation of the Jina image in private houses and speak of the household shrines. Hariṣeṇa in his *Padmapurāṇa* states[1] that the people should install Jina image in their houses and worship it. The absence of Jina icons in any Jaina house is said to have brought misery to the devotee. On the other hand, the house which contains the Jina image is thought to be free from the influence of evil spirits. He further states the story of a Jaina woman, who had to suffer the separation of her husband for a long time in her next life, because she had dishonoured the Jina in her private house.[2]

Jinasena in his *Ādipurāṇa* advises the Jainas not to worship the deities of the other faiths in their private homes.[3] It proves beyond doubt that the Jainas in Karnataka keep the Jina image for personal adoration. He also informs us that the Jainas used to hang a bell, containing the Jina image, at the main entrance to their houses so that they may always offer salutation to him.[4] At another place, he speaks of the household shrines which seem to have been situated within the compound of the palaces of kings, where worship was probably performed for the whole family.[5] There is nothing to show that the neighbouring Jainas were not permitted to visit such temples for worship. All this proves the prevalence of private temple worship among the Jainas in Karnataka. It also seems reasonable to assume that the Jaina idols were worshipped on communal, family and individual basis during the early medieval age.

Daily worship of the Jina in Jaina temples

An important custom of the Jainas was their daily attendance in the Jaina temples for the worship of the Jinas. It

1. *Padmapurāṇa*, pt. iii, ch. 92, v. 73ff.. p. 181.
2. Ibid. pt. i, ch. 17, v. 165ff., pp. 382-3.
3. *Ādipurāṇa,* pt. ii, ch. 39, v. 45ff, p. 273.
4. Ibid. pt. ii, ch. 41, v. 87ff, p. 324.
5. Ibid. pt. i, ch. 5, v. 227ff, p. 113.

consisted in morning and evening worship of the Jinas. The Jaina *purāṇas* and other literary texts of Karnataka emphasise the need of observing some preliminary religious rites before the performance of the actual worship of the Jinas. These include bathing, expiation and circumambulation, which all are deemed essential for maintaining the purity of mind and body of the worshippers. Somadeva[1] in his *Yaśastilaka* refers to the internal and external purity of the Jainas. By internal purity, he means purity of mind. The need of taking bath in pure water and washing of the teeth are included in external purity. He warns the Jainas against the use of hot water[2] for bathing because of the fear of injury to living creatures.

The expiatory rite of the Jainas is also an important preliminary ritual. The Jaina devotees are said to have got rid of the impurity caused by their movements on their way to their temples. Jinasena explains it as the *īrya-patha-śuddhikriyā*.[3] Both the monks and laymen are asked to observe it in order to absolve themselves of the acts of sin.

In the circumambulation rite (*pradakṣiṇā*) the Jaina devotees walk round the Jaina temples thrice[4] before performing acts of worship, and the same rite is repeated after the final act of the Jina worship.[5] For this rite circumambulatory passages were provided in the Jaina temples.

The *Yaśastilaka*[6] throws light on the different stages of Jaina worship. The first stage is formed by the *prastāvanā* (prelude), which means the summoning of the Jina and making preparations for his worship.[7] It is followed by the *purākarma*, which is the purification of the place of worship and the establishment of water vessels over it on the occasion of ablution ceremony.[8] The third stage is the formal placing of the

1. *Yaśastilaka*, pt. ii, BK. viii, pp. 372-3.
2. Ibid.
3. *Ādipurāṇa*, pt. i, ch. 7, vv. 275-6, p. 162.
4. *Varāṅgacarita*, ch. 23, v. 57, p. 225.
5. *Harivaṁśapurāṇa*, pt. i, ch. 22, v. 44, p. 334.
6. *Yaśastilaka*, pt. ii, BK. viii, pp. 382ff.
7. Ibid.
8. Ibid. p. 383.

Jina idol on the altar, and is called *sthāpanā*.[1] The installation of Jina images is frequently referred to in the epigraphs. An epigraph of 1138[2] speaks of installation ceremony of the god Mallinātha in the Dinkar Jinālaya at Bastihaḷḷi in the Belur taluq. Similar evidence is available from other inscriptions which refer to the installation of the images of Neminātha,[3] Pārśvanātha[4] and Cenna-Pārśvanātha[5] in the middle of the 12th century. The *sannidhāpana* is the act of going nearest to the Jina, which is expressed in a highly eulogistic manner.[6] The study of the verses composed by Somadeva gives the impression of spiritual flattery to the Jina. *Pūjā* or the worship proper comprised the actual ablution ceremony, waving of lamp (*āratī*), offerings of eight articles and recitation of Jaina hymns before the idol.

The Karnataka Jaina texts also enlighten us about the various acts of the Jina worship, which are invariably performed in every Jaina temple. The bathing rite of the Jina appears to be the most important act of worship. The *Varāṅgacarita*[7] provides the most detailed description of the bathing ritual. It lays emphasis on the maintenance of purity. The devotees are advised to observe complete fast and to take bath before proceeding to the performance of Jina ablution. They are also said to have put on white cloth, which indicates cleanliness in matters relating to clothing.[8] The devotees collect waters from holy rivers, wells, fountains and pilgrim places and store them in four earthen pitchers. The water pitchers are beautifully decorated with flowers and are carried by the devotees to the Jaina temples.[9] As soon as they enter the temple, they perform circumambulation thrice and proceed towards the *abhiṣeka-śālā* or the ablution hall. In the ablution hall, the Jaina priest, known as the *snapanācārya* (the priest)

1. *Yaśastilaka*, pt. ii, BK. viii, pp. 312-3.
2. *EC*, xv, p. 5.
3. *MAR*, 1944, p. 43.
4. *EC*, iv, Ng. 94. p. 138.
5. Ibid. v, Hn 57, p. 16.
6. *Yaśastilaka*, pt. ii, BK. viii, p. 383.
7. *Varāṅgacarita*, ch. 23, v. 58ff. pp. 225ff.
8. Ibid. vv. 32-4, p. 223.
9. Ibid, vv. 23ff, p. 222.

for bathing), is employed for performing the bathing rite.[1] He brings the Jina idol from the inner shrine and places it on the high altar in the hall of ablution. He then takes a vow to keep silence till the end of the ceremony. He installs the image on a stone pedestal, which is corroborated by an epigraph of the 10th century ; it informs us that the Rāṣṭrakūṭa King Nityavarṣa constructed a stone seat for the bath of the image of Śāntinātha.[2] Two other epigraphs, which are dated in 1138[3] and 1182[4] record gifts of land for the performance of bathing ritual of the Jinas in the 12th century. After the installation of the Jina on the stone seat, the priest performs salutation by prostrating himself. He first discharges water in a continuous flow on the feet of Jinendra, standing in the north direction, and dries it so carefully that no drop of water falls on the ground. He utters a Jaina formula and makes offerings. Thereafter he performs the ablution of the head of the Jina by continuously pouring water over the image, which is known as the *mastakābhiṣeka*.[5] It is followed by the offerings of flowers, unbroken rice, sandal, fruit, etc., to *dikpālas* (guardian deities of different directions) and *kṣetrapālas*. After the performance of these acts, the priest performs *āratī* with lamp and breaks his vow of silence.[6]

Somadeva[7] gives additional information about the bathing rite. He states that the idol is bathed with fragrant water, clarified butter, the juice of vines, dates, sugarcanes and coconut milk. Four pitchers filled with water and decorated with flowers are kept ready for the bathing ritual of the Jina.

The anointing ceremony of the Jina is the next act of the Jaina worship. The deity is anointed with various pastes and compounds made of sandal, aloe wood and cardamoms.[8]

1. *Varāṅgacarita*, ch. 23, v. 58, p. 225.
2. *SII*, ix, pt i, p. 36.
3. *EC*, ii. SB 402, p. 170.
4. Ibid. vii, pp. 124-7.
5. *Varāṅgacarita*, ch. 23, v. 62ff., p. 226ff.
6. Ibid, v. 68ff., p. 226.
7. K.K. Handiqui, op. cit. p. 270.
8. Ibid. p. 270.

Numerous inscriptions refer to the performance of the anointing ceremony of the Jina in the Jaina temples. In one epigraph, Mṛigeśavarmā is said to have donated a field of forty *nivartanas* for the purpose of anointing the Jina idol with ghee.[1] Another record speaks of the provision made by the king of the same house for perpetual anointment of the Jina with clarified butter.[2] Inscriptions, belonging to 11th-12th centuries, also contain informations regarding the anointing ceremony of the Jinas. They register grants of land and village for the observance of this ritual.[3] Mariyānedaṇḍanāyaka, a general of the Hosyaḷa period, is said to have rejoiced in the daily anointing ceremony of the Jina in Jaina temple.[4]

Iyer observes[5] that there is no decoration of the idol either with flowers or jewellery. But it is difficult to agree with him. That the Jina image was decorated with flowers and garlands is well illustrated in the *Varāṅgacarita*. It informs us that the priest offered beautiful garlands to the Jinas.[6]

It is also corroborated by the Jaina records right from the 6th century to the 12th century. A record, which is dated in the 6th century[7], refers to a grant of land of one *nivartana* for decorating the idol with rich flowers. In 1096 Sovi Seṭṭi gave a gift of a garden to Cārukīrti-Paṇḍita of the Yāpanīya Saṅgha.[8] For the Jaina temple in Bannikere in the Shimoga district, Bācaladevī also donated a garden in 1113.[9] Puṇisa, who was a general of the Hoysaḷa king, is recorded to have decorated the *basadi* of the Gaṅgavāḍi 96,000 in 1117.[10] Besides the above instances, Śravaṇa-

1. *IA*, vii, no. 36. p. 36.
2. Ibid. vi, no. 25, p. 31 ; *EC*, viii, Sh. 114, p. 37.
3. *EC*, vii, Sk. 124, p. 170 ; ibid. viii, Sh. 140, p. 20.
4. Ibid. vi, Cm. 160, p. 57.
5. Ananthakrishna Iyer, *The Mysore Tribes and Castes*, iii, p. 436.
6. *Varāṅgacarita*, ch. 23, v. 66. p. 226.
7. *IA*, vii, no, 36, p. 36.
8. *BKI*, i, no. 140, p. 169.
9. *EC*, vii. Sh. 97, pp. 35-6.
10. Ibid. iv, ch. 83, p. 10.

Beḷgoḷa epigraphs give us additional information about the offerings of flowers and garlands to the Jinas and Gommaṭeśvara on the Vindhyagiri hill.[1] In one of the Śravaṇa-Beḷgoḷa epigraphs, there is specific reference to garland-makers, who were given land for regular supply of garlands to Gommaṭeśvara in 1175.[2] It becomes obvious from the above records that the Digambaras in Karnataka devoted special attention to the decoration of the Jina-idols. In order to fulfil their objects, they not only granted land and village but also the garden itself. Besides, they gave land to the garland-makers for the regular supply of flowers. Thus, the Jaina temples in Karnataka seem to have employed garland-makers, who were maintained at the cost of Jaina devotees.

The ritual of worship seems to have been followed by *japa* or repeated recitation of the sacred Jaina syllables, consisting of thirty-five letters. The devotees visualized a mental image of the Jina and worshipped him with the help of the *mantra* and *mudrā* (symbolic gestures). Somadeva in his *Yaśastilaka* stresses the importance of the contemplation of the mystic formula. He advises the Jainas to meditate on the *oṁkāra* formula, mentally locating it on the top of the nose, and so concentrate the mind on space between eye brows. He should arouse the mystic lotus inside his navel and move the connected artery and then direct the four winds or subtle breaths relating to earth, water, fire and air towards the mind.[3] The emphasis on the efficacy of the *japa* is also found in the *Ādipurāṇa*. Jinasena points out the various good results obtained by the Jaina devotees. They are said to have obtained not only the desired things but also the final deliverance from the cycle of rebirths through its proper recitation.[4] Somadeva, too, explains its mystic value by stating that any one who mentally repeats it attains all kinds of prosperity.[5] The Jaina practice of *japa* appears to be an imitation of the Brāhmaṇical

1. *EC*, ii, SB 237, p. 101 ; SB 238, p. 101 ; SB 241, p. 103.
2. Ibid. ii, SB 242, pp. 103-4.
3. K.K. Handiqui, op. cit. p. 280.
4. *Ādipurāṇa*, pt. ii, ch. 21, v. 231ff, p. 489,
5. K.K. Handiqui, op. cit. p. 280.

injunctions which prescribe the muttering of Vedic mantra for atoning all kinds of sin and attaining happiness. The utterance of the sacred Jaina hymns completes the final acts of temple rituals. The devotees then bow down before the Jina idol and leave the temple after performing the circumambulation rite.

The evening worship of the Jina seems to have included the performance of *āratī*, in which the lamp was revolved in a circular fashion before the idol. Then the Jainas offered *homa* and burnt incense before the Jina.[1] As the Jainas consider the taking of food after sunset an act of sin, they did not offer food to the Jina at night.

Jaṭila's reference to the performance of music and dance in the Jaina temples[2] shows that music and dance formed an important item of the evening worship. Ravisena too highly commends the performance of music and dance as meritorious act for the laymen. The devotee is said to have gained eternal bliss as a result of his arrangement for dance and music in Jaina temples.[3] The popularity of dance is also attested by an epigraph of the 9th century. It states that the Rāṣṭrakūṭa king gave a gift of the village to provide for dancers and drummers.[4] Probably the temple employed professional dancers for the performance of the temple ritual and paid some remuneration to them. This pactice led to the origin of the institution of *devadāsīs* or temple prostitutes in later times.

The *āṣṭāhnika pūjā* or the eight-day's worship of the Jina in the Jaina temples was a kind of periodical worship. Both the literary and epigraphic sources speak of its prevalence among the Jainas in Karnataka. The epigraphs refer to its performance in the Jaina temples and the Jaina texts frcm Karnataka throw light on the method, time and rituals adopted by the Jaina.

The worship was performed thrice in a year in the months of Phālguṇa (February-March), Āṣāḍha (June-July)

1. *Varāṅgacarita*, ch. 23, v. 70, p. 226.
2. Ibid. v. 10, p. 221.
3. *Padmapurāṇa*, pt. ii, ch. 32, v. 171, p. 98.
4. *EC*, ix. NL. 61, pp. 44-5.

and Kārttika (October-November). It commenced from the 8th day of the bright fortnight and closed with the full moon day.[1] The selection of a particular month and time shows the influence of the Hindu calendar upon the Jainas. They consider these eight days as auspicious. Ravisena[2] tells us that the devotees spared time for its grand celebration in the Jaina temples. They decorated the temple with utmost care and made arrangements for music and dance on this occasion. As they are supposed to lead the life of an ascetic during these days, Ravisena advises them to abstain from any act of *hiṁsā* (injury to living creatures).[3]

The worshippers attended daily the Jina temple in order to perform the ablution ceremony of the Jina with ghee, milk and water. Fasting during these eight-days seems to have been an important element in this worship.[4] The Jainas spent their remaining time in the study and recitation of the Jaina scriptures. Recitation may have contributed to the popularization of Jainism among the people. The devotees left the temple after the evening worship and practised charity according to their means.[5]

Emergence of priest class in Karnataka

The increasing popularity of image worship led to the rise of priests in the early medieval period. The *Varāṅgacarita* speaks and calls them *snapanācārya*[6] and *pratiṣṭhācārya.*[7] The two terms show that they performed temple rituals connected with the worship of the Jina. The *snapanācārya* performed the bathing rite of the Jina, and the *pratiṣṭhācārya* installed the idol on the altar and made available articles of worship in the Jaina temples. The term *gṛihasthācārya*[8] is also mentioned, and stands for the Jaina priest who performed the domestic rites on behalf of the lay men. He was obviously far more important

1. *Padmapurāṇa*, pt. iii, ch. 68, v. 1, p. 12.
2. Ibid. pt. ii, ch. 29, vv. 3-6, p. 45.
3. Ibid. pt. iii, ch. 68, v. 4, p. 12 ; ibid. pt. *i*, ch. 22, v. 132, p. 467.
4. Ibid. pt. ii, ch. 29, v. 8, p. 45.
5. *Varāṅgacarita*, ch. 15, v. 140ff, pp. 140-1.
6. Ibid. ch. 23, v. 58, p. 225.
7. Ibid. v. 22ff. p. 222.
8. Ibid. v. 84ff, p, 228.

than the other two types of priests, and occupied an important position in the Jaina social and religious order.

The Jaina epigraphs of the 5th-6th centuries provide further information about the priests. Kākutsthavarmā is recorded to have donated a field in the village Kheṭagrāma to the general Śrutakīrti, who saved his life from some danger.[1] Śrutakīrti is described as *bhoja* in a record of the Kadamba king Ravivarmā.[2] Dāmakīrti, son of Śrutakīrti, is referred to as *bhojaka* in several epigraphs.[3] Similar is the case with Paṇḍara, who is designated as *bhojaka*.[4] The term *bhoja* is explained as a class of priests, supposed to be descended from the Magas by inter-marriage with the women of the *bhoja* race.[5] Thus, the epithet *bhoja* or *bhojaka* applied to Śrutakīrti, Dāmakīrti and Paṇḍara, refer especially to a class of officiating priests in the Jaina temple at Palāśika or modern Halsi in the district of Belgaum. Śrutakīrti, although described as a general under the Kadamba king Kakutsthavarmā, held the offices of priest and commander. He, thus, may be regarded as the predecessor of the priestly family which flourished in Karnataka during the 5th-6th centuries.

The office of the priest sometimes passed from father to the son, but did not become hereditary. Jayakīrti, who was the son of a Jaina priest Dāmākīrti, acted as the door-keeper (pratihārī).[6] In other respects, the Jaina priests resembled the brāhmaṇical priests. They functioned as householders. Śrutakīrti, who was the progenitor of the priestly family, was a married person. The wife of Śrutakīrti is also said to have received a grant of land from the Kadamba king Śāntivarmā and his son Mṛigeśvarmā.[7]

The term *bhoja* or *bhojaka*, which stands for the priest class in Karnataka, is not mentioned in later records. Since

1. *IA*, vi, no 20. p. 24.
2. Ibid. no. 22, p. 27.
3. Ibid. no. 21, p. 25 ; *IA*, vii, no. 36, p. 36.
4. Ibid. no. 23, p. 29.
5. Monier-Williams, *A Sanskrit English Dictionary*, p. 768.
6. *IA*, vi, no. 22, pp. 26-7.
7. Ibid.

the middle of the 7th-8th centuries, inscriptions do not furnish any information about the continuation of the *bhoja* priests. They generally refer to the term *ācārya*, who is entrusted with the task of supervising the affairs of Jaina monasteries and temples. In most of the records, the same dignitary has been declared as the recipient of gifts for discharging functions relating to Jina worship and monastic organisation such as the maintenance of monks and nuns residing in monasteries, the proper control of charity-houses and fair distribution of alms. In 683 the Cālukya king Vinayāditya donated a village for repairs, worship and offerings to the god Śaṅkha-Jinendra and maintaining a dāna-śālā at the request of Dhurvadevācārya of the Mūla saṅgha and the Deva gaṇa.[1] Jayadevapaṇḍitācārya of the Mūla saṅgha received a gift of the village Sembolal in 723 on behalf of the Jaina temple at Puligere or Lakṣameśvara in the Dharwar district.[2] In 734-35 Śrīvijayadevapaṇḍitācārya of the Devagaṇa received a gift so that he could make necessary provision for the repairs of the temple and the maintenance of the alms houses attached to the Śaṅkhatīrtha *basadi* at Lakṣmeśvara in the same district.[3] The donative records of the 9th-10th centuries give similar information and do not distinguish between the Jaina monks and priests.

In the middle of the 11th century, Nāgasenapaṇḍita of the Hogari gaccha of the Mūla saṅgha was given land for the maintenance of the establishment of the monks and nuns, attached to it, for supply of scent, incense and lamp to the Goṇaḍa Beḍaṅgi Jinālaya at Vikramapura[4] in the Hungund taluq of the Bijapur district. In the 12th century, Nayakīrti-Siddhānta Cakravarti, the ācārya of the Śrī Mūla saṅgha, Deśiya gaṇa, Pustaka gaccha and Kondakundānvaya, is said to have received land in order to provide the eight kinds of ceremonies, for a repair of the Pārśvanātha Jaina temple and the distribution of food to the ascetics during the rule of the Hoysaḷa king Narasiṁhadeva.[5] In the last quarter of the same

1. *BKI*, iv, no. 4, p. 3.
2. Ibid. no. 5, p. 4.
3. *IA*. vii, no. 38, 109ff ; *BKI*, iv, no. 7, p. 7.
4. *EI*, xvii, no. 10, pp. 121-3.
5. *EC*, v, Hn. 67, p. 16.

century, the Hoysaḷa king gave gift of the village Marikali for Trikūṭa Jinālaya in the Hassan district. It was made over to Vasupūjya Siddhāntadeva, disciple of Śrīpālatraividya-deva of the Arungalānvaya and the Dramila saṅgha.[1] In another record, which is dated in 1133,[2] Prabhācandra-Saiddhāntika, the ācārya of the Gaṅgamaṇḍala, was Boppa-deva's guru for divine worship. Boppadeva is said to have erected a fine Jaina temple in Dorasamudra as a memorial to Gaṅga Rāja and set up the image of the god Pārśva, which was consecrated by Nayakīrti-Siddhāntacakravartī. After its consecration, Nayakīrtisiddhāntacakravartī took the consecrated food to Viṣṇuvardhana at Bankapur. Viṣṇu-vardhana being filled with joy on account of both his victory in the battlefield and the birth of a son, gave warm reception to him and granted the village Jāvagal for the repairs of the Vijaya-Pārśva Jaina temple and Gaṅganūr for the decorations and the maintenance of the learned.

In the above records, recipients of gifts were evidently Jaina monks, who probably held both the offices of priests and monks. It became difficult to draw a line of distinction between the two in later times because of the combined structure of Jaina monasteries and temples. The Jaina monastery in Karnataka was generally a composite structure, incorporating both monasteries and temples within it. As some of the later epigraphs refer to the appointment of Jaina monks[3] for wor-

1. *EC*, Hn. 119, p. 35.
2. Ibid. Bl. 124, pp. 82-3.
3. *EI*. vi, no. 4, A.D. 860, pp. 35-8; *EC*, ii, SB 345, A.D 1159, pp. 147-9. Nayakīrti, Siddhānta-Cakravartī is said to have been made an ācārya of the Caturviṁśati-Tīrthaṅkara Jaina temple near Gommaṭa-pura on the Vindhyagiri hill by the Hoysaḷa general Huḷḷa; *EC*, viii, Ng. 40, A.D. 1087, pp. 144-5; Ajitasenapaṇḍitācārya is said to have been appointed by Vikrama Śāntara-Deva as the chief of the ascetic congregation of the Dramila gaṇa, Nandi Saṅgha and Arungalānvaya. He was given grants of village for the worship at the Pañcakūṭa *basadi* in the Shimoga district. *EC*, v, Cn. 146, A.D. 1174, pp. 188-9. The Hoysaḷa king Vīra-Ballāla appointed Bhānukīrti Siddhānta-cakravartī as the manager of the god Pārśva and Gommaṭatīrtha.

shipping the Jina images, it seems possible to infer that there emerged a class of priests from among the monks who took part in the celebration of worship rituals.

The reasons which impelled them to adopt the profession of priest are not difficult to find out. The rise of hedonistic tendencies and slack practices and the lust for material gains among the Jaina monks would have forced them to encroach upon the rights of priest class which prevailed in Karnataka during the 5th-6th centuries. Thus, the distinction between Jaina monks and priests gradually disappeared from the 7th-8th centuries. The change in the usual practice of priesthood would have surely made them the sole master of enormous wealth, acquired from endowments made by the Jaina devotees.

The above analysis of the nature of Jaina monks in Karnataka shows how far they departed from the precepts of their founder Mahāvīra, who denounced the infallible authority of the priest class among the Hindus and laid emphasis on the purity of soul rather than the observances of ritualistic formalism. The rituals introduced by the Jaina teachers of Karnataka were not in keeping with the original puritan character of Jainism. The introduction of rituals also affected the Jaina vow of *ahiṁsā* (non-injury). In the course of performing worship and rituals, the Jaina devotees occasionally committed acts of injury to unseen germs in water, flowers, etc., which were used in the worship of the Jina. The offering of *homa* or fire oblation and *āratī* or waving the lamp round the Jina killed small insects.

Jaina Goddesses and their Association with Tantrism

The worship of mother goddesses appeared as an entirely new phenomenon among the Jainas of Karnataka during early medieval times. The elevation of some Jaina Yakṣiṇīs from the minor deities to a superior position formed the basis of the mother cult in Karnataka.

The Yakṣiṇīs, who figure most prominently in the early Jaina literature, were a class of attendant deities and had no separate existence apart from the Jinas. Their position underwent considerable change during this period. They were now deified and worshipped among the Jainas as independent divinities. The exaltation of their position is evident from several factors. In iconic representations of the 7th century, Ambikā or Kūṣmāṇḍinī, who is the Yakṣiṇī of the 22nd Jina, is given four arms with two children in her lap. She is depicted on the left side of the Jina as waiting upon her lord.[1] But the Yakṣiṇī of the Meguṭi temple at Aihoḷe in the Bijapur district, who is identified with Ambikā or Ambādevī, does not wait upon the Jina but is shown independently. She does not carry any children herself; instead the children are held by two lady attendants on either side.[2]

The changes in the usual position of the Yakṣiṇīs, who were originally placed invariably on the left side of the Jina,[3] also attest their elevation. The image of the Yakṣiṇī, which has been found in the cave temple at Badami, is depicted on the right side of the 7th Jina Supārśvanātha. The representation of this female is important, for, unlike the Yakṣiṇīs, she is holding no particular symbols in her two hands.[4] Thus, the cave no. 5 (A.D. 750-950) at Badami indicates the higher status of the Yakṣiṇīs.

The exaltation of the position of the Yakṣiṇīs is also evident from their iconographical representations in other regions beside Mysore. The two images of Padmāvatī, which have been found at Hanumānkoṇḍa and Dānavulapāḍu in Andhra Pradesh, give us the same impression. The image of Padmākṣī, who is identified with the Jaina Yakṣiṇī Padmāvatī, is clearly on the right side of the Jina.[5] In the Tamil region the Anandamangalam sculptures,[6] which belong to the 9th-10th centuries, place the Yakṣiṇī Siddhāyikā on the right side of the 24th Jina Mahāvīra.

1. Jas Burgess, *Digambara Jaina Iconography*, p. 5. Also see, *IA*, xxxii, p. 463.
2. Henry Cousens, *The Chalukyan Architecture of the Kanarese districts*, p, 31.
3. Cf. Figures of the Yakṣiṇīs, Plates i-iv.
4. *BDCRI*, i, pp. 160-1.
5. Gopalkrishna Murthy, *Jaina Vestiges in Andhra Pradesh*, pp. 27-31.
6. P. B. Desai, *op. cit.*, p. 38.

The Jaina preceptors, who contributed to the development of the Yakṣiṇī cult in Karnataka, seem to have concentrated their attention on the worship of some particular Yakṣiṇīs. Of the important secondary deities who were promoted to a higher position, Jvālāmālinī, Padmāvatī and Ambikā emerged as the most popular goddesses and received public adoration of the Jainas in Karnataka.

Jvālāmālinī, who is the Yakṣiṇī of the 8th Jina Candraprabha[1], is described as the goddess of fire in the Digambara tradition.[2] This is proved by the burning blazes of flames issuing upward from her crest. The *Jvālinī-kalpa*, which was composed by Indranandi in the 10th century, also describes her as the *agnivāhinidevī* or the goddess of fire.[3] She appears to be a terrible deity, who has eight arms carrying deadly weapons such as arrow, shield, trident, bow, snake, etc.[4]

The *Jvālinī-kalpa* gives an interesting story of the beginning of this cult. It states that Helācārya of the famous Draviḍa Saṅgha first started her worship on the summit of the Nilgiri hill near Hemagrāma in the south in order to remove the bad influence of an evil spirit, known as *Brahmarākṣasa* who had overpowered his lady disciple Kamalaśrī.[5] After continuous meditation for a number of days he succeeded on the 7th day, when the goddess appeared and asked him to write an incantation on a sheet of iron to emancipate her from the influence of evil spirit.[6] She also advised him to systematise the occult practices for achieving all the earthly and heavenly blessings.

The event, which is narrated in the text, cannot be assigned any definite date. Probably, it happened in the middle of the 9th century, for Indranandi, who finally composed this text in 939 at the Rāṣṭrakūṭa capital Mālkheḍ, was the fifth Jaina teacher who succeeded Helācārya. Indranandi is said to have learnt this system from Kandarpa and Guṇanandi. It

1. Jas Burgess, op. cit. p. 4; *IA*, xxxii, p. 462.
2. Ibid. Fig. 8, Plate ii.
3. *Jvālinī-Kalpa*, ch. 1, v. 2, p. 1.
4. Ibid.
5. Ibid. vv. 5-7, p. 1.
6. Ibid. vv. 8ff. pp. 1-2.

further states that Guṇanandi was preceded by Nīlgrīva and Gaṅgamuni.[1] Of these two, the latter was a direct disciple of Helācārya.[2] If we allot only 20 years for each generation of teachers, we may safely place Helācārya during the middle of the 9th century which marked the beginning of the worship of Jvālāmālinī in Karnataka.

The composition of the *Jvālinī-Kalpa* by Indranandi during the middle of the 10th century led to the popularity of this goddess. We have epigraphic evidence to show the prevalence of her worship in Karnataka in the 11th-12th centuries. A temple was constructed for Jvālāmālinī at Jāvur in Navalgunda taluq of the Dharwar district sometime before 1059.[3] It was erected by a monk of the Yāpanīya sect evidently for offering independent worship. The Yāpanīya sect of the Jainas in Mysore took great care for propagating the idea of tantric worship and for glorifying the tantric attributes of Jaina goddesses. This led to the spread of the cult in other regions. Seḍam or modern Sedam in the Gulbarga district was another important centre of the Jvālāmālinī cult, as can be inferred from an epigraph of 1124 which states that the local *mahājanas* or merchants performed exorcising rites in order to please Jvālinī. She is described as goddess Jvālinī wearing golden ear-rings.[4] Besides the above centres, Eḍehaḷḷi or Narasimharajapura in the Kadur district and Veḍgaon in the Kolhapur area were other places where Jvālāmālinī received public adoration.[5]

Padmāvatī, the guardian deity of the 23rd Jina Pārśvanātha[6] was another popular goddess of the Jainas in Karnataka. She figures in the story of the foundation of the Gaṅga kingdom in the second century, and is said to have favoured Mādhava with a magic sword for breaking a pillar. But there are grave doubts regarding the origin of her cult at

1. *Jvālinī Kalpa*, vv. 20ff., pp. 2-3.
2. *Ibid.*
3. P.B. Desai, *op. cit* , p. 143.
4. *Ibid.*, pp. 259-61.
5. *Ibid.*, p. 173.
6. Jas Burgess, *op. cit*, p. 5; *IA*, xxxii, p. 463.

such an early age, because this tradition appears in the epigraphs of the 11th-12th centuries. However, the Yakṣiṇī Padmāvatī, who figures frequently in the records of the Śāntara kings, gained prominence in Karnataka as a cult goddess from the 10th century. Jinadatta Rāya, the founder of the Śāntara kingdom in the south, is recorded to have set up Lokkiyabbe in the Jaina temple at Paṭṭi-Pombuccapura or modern Humcca[1] in the Nagar taluq of the Shimoga district in the 10th century. That Lokkiyabbe was the second name of Padmāvatī is known from another record of the 11th century.[2] In the first quarter of the twelfth century, Nanniya Gaṅgadeva and his queen Kancaladevī are recorded to have granted five *paṇas* for the goddess Padmāvatī.[3] Besides the Śāntara kings, a large number of minor ruling families such as the Śilāhāras and the Raṭṭas became votaries of this goddess in the 11th-12th centuries.[4] How the worship of the goddess Padmāvatī had penetrated deep into Karnataka society, is illustrated by the adoption of her names by the people of Karnataka. Padmāvatiyakka, for example, was the name of a lady, who is described as a lady disciple of the priest Abhayacandra.[5]

Ambikā or Kūṣmāṇḍinī, the Yakṣiṇī of the 22nd Jina,[6] also attained independent status by the middle of the 7th century. It is proved by the figure of the Yakṣiṇī in the Meguṭi temple at Aihoḷe in the Bijapur district.[7] In the 8th century Akalaṅka is said to have vanquished his Buddhist opponents by invoking the aid of Kūṣmāṇḍinī. Somadeva refers to the prevalence of her cult in the 10th century.[8] Thus it is clear that some of the Jaina Yakṣiṇīs, who were the deities of a minor order, acquired all the characteristics of independent divinities among the Jainas of Karnataka.

1. *EC*, vii, Sh 114, p. 37.
2. Ibid. viii, Nr 35, p. 134.
3. Ibid. vii, Sh 4, pp. 4-9.
4. P.B. Desai, op. cit., p. 171.
5. *MAR*, 1926, p. 42, cited in B.A. Saletore, op. cit. pp. 157-8.
6. *IA*, xxxii, p. 463.
7. Henry Cousens, op. cit. p. 31.
8. P.B. Desai, op. cit. p. 173.

Gradually tantric attributes and tantric rites were associated with these Yakṣiṇīs. They are said to have bestowed superhuman powers upon the devotees by which the latter could bring a person under control, win over the enemies on the battlefield and cause hostility between two persons. The element of magic and miracle, which was attributed to Jvālāmālinī and Padmāvatī, is evident from the study of the Jaina texts on tantrism.

The growth of the Jaina tantrism was the natural outcome of the early medieval age, which witnessed the infiltration of tantrism into Buddhism, Śaivism and Vaiṣṇavism. In this age the people in general relied more upon the supernatural agencies for the fulfilment of temporal as well as spiritual ideals. They abandoned the original ethical principles for the sake of mysterious yogic practices and magical spells. The Jaina preceptors of Karnataka, who advocated the worship of tantric deities, were thus no exception to the prevailing religious norms. They made full use of magical spells and amulets, and systematised the occult lore in their works.

The spread of occult practices among the Jainas of Karnataka was not a sudden development, for they first appear in the early Jaina texts. Despite the denunciation of these customs in the Jaina scriptures, the Jainas practised incantation from earliest times. The *Sthānāṅgasūtra* refers to the Jainas who were sensualists.[1] The curative spells are mentioned in the *Uttarādhyayana Sūtra*.[2] In the *Sūtrakṛtāṅga*,[3] we have instances of the monks who take to incantation for making a person happy or miserable. The *Niryuktis*, which are assigned to 300-500,[4] state that the Jaina monks managed to acquire food with the help of magical spells.[5] The *Samarāiccakahā*, which is a work of the 8th century, refers to a magician who restored life to Sagaradatta who was administered

1. The *Sthānāṅgasūtra*, 4.4, cited in Chintaharan Chakravarti, *Tantras-Studies on their Religion and Literature*, p. 16,
2. Ibid.
3. Ibid.
4. S.B. Deo, op. cit., p. 42.
5. Ibid. p. 298.

strong poison by his mother.[1] In the same text, we have the story of a goddess who gave Sena a miraculous stone which could remove all diseases. With this he cured king Samaraketu of his disease when all physicians had failed.[2]

The epigraphs of our period also speak of the supernatural powers of the Jaina monks. According to a 7th century epigraph[3] from Śravaṇa-Beḷgoḷa, Bhadrabāhu forecast a calamity in the North. The Jaina monk Arkakīrti received a grant of land and village for removing the influence of an evil spirit from a prince named Vimalāditya during the reign of the Rāṣṭrakūṭa king Govinda III.[4]

Though we have several instances of magical spells and charms in much earlier times, a fully developed system of Jaina tantrism was evolved in Karnataka in the 10th-11th centuries. The Jaina preceptors made valuable contributions to the growth of tantric literature and systematised the occult lore in their works.

The composition of the *Jvālinī-Kalpa* by Indranandi and the *Bhairava Padmāvatī-Kalpa* by Mallisena Sūri, which are mainly devoted to the glorification of Jvālāmālinī and Padmāvatī, marked the perfection of the Jaina tantric system, which now assimilated almost all the main characteristics of tantrism, such as *mantras* or the utterance of fixed syllabic words, *yantra* or mechanical contrivances drawn on paper or inscribed on precious stone, metal, etc., for obtaining favourable results, *mudrās* or special positions of fingers and movements of hands, and the *nyāsa* or imaginary placing of the deities on the different parts of the body. These are the means by which the aspirant invokes and identifies himself with his chosen deity.[5]

The tantric character of these goddesses is evident from the study of the above two treatises, which laid down ins-

1. *Samarāicca-Kahā*, pp. 153, 79, cited in *JA*, viii, no. 1, p. 23.
2. Ibid. pp. 564-8, cited in *JA*, viii, no. 1, p. 22.
3. *EC*, ii, SB. 1, p. 1.
4. *EC*, xii, Gb. 61, pp. 30-1;
   EI, iv, no. 49, p. 349.
5. R. C. Mazumdar, (ed.), *The Age of Imperial Kanauj*, (First edition), p. 317.

tructions for the observance of the tantric rites. The *Padmāvatī-Kalpa*, for example, refers to the observance of the six magical rites[1] for the attainment of the desired results.

The *Padmāvatī-Kalpa* devotes one chapter to the rites relating to *vaśīkaraṇa* or *vaśyatantrādhikara*,[2] and lays down tantric formulas and mystic diagrams for invoking the aid of the goddess Padmāvatī. Chapter 9 of this text explains the tantric methods by which a woman can be easily overpowered.[3] The other magical rites such as *stambhana* or the rite of making one motionless, *dveṣa* or the art of causing enmity, and *śānti* or the rites performed with a view to removing calamity and disease, are referred to in both the *Bhairava Padmāvatī-Kalpa* and the *Jvālinī-Kalpa*.

Of these two texts, the former teaches the aspiring devotees the appropriate methods and insists on the correct knowledge of different directions, time, bodily postures and special positions of fingers and movements of hands for attaining success.[4] It recommends the observance of *sarojamudrā* and *svastikāsana* for the performance of the rite of *vaśikaraṇa* in the morning of the spring season.[5]

The utterance of *mantras*, which has a special significance in the tantric form of worship, is also referred to in the *Bhairava-Padmāvatī-Kalpa*. It lays down[6] that the devotee should repeatedly utter the *mantra* and offer oblation to the fire, enkindled before the goddess. He is enjoined to give 1/10th of his time to offering oblations to the fire. In order to please the goddess Padmāvatī, the devotees are advised to repeat the *mantra* known as the *kliṅkāramantra*. It also mentions a mystic formula, which, if uttered one lakh times, causes sleep to the enemy.[7] Though the vast majority of the *mantras* uttered for invoking the goddesses carry no sense such as *hrīṅ*, *huṅ*, *hrāṁ*, *hruṁ hraḥ*, and *vaṁ*, *maṁ*, *haṁ*, *saṁ*, *taṁ*, etc., they are

1. *Bhairava-Padmāvatī-Kalpa*, ch. 3, v. 1, p. 9.
2. Ibid. ch. 7, pp. 36-44.
3. Ibid. ch. 9, pp. 53-61.
4. Ibid. ch. 3, v. 4. p. 9.
5. Ibid. v. 5ff, pp. 9-10.
6. Ibid. v. 4, p. 9.
7. Ibid. ch. 7, v. 23, p. 41.

supposed to produce beneficial results for the worshippers.

The performance of the *nyāsa* or consecrating the different parts of the body with the names of the deity is another important tantric rite. We come across a detailed description of this rite known as *svāṅgavinyāsa* in the chapter called *sakalīkaraṇa*.[1] It refers to the purification of the head, face, heart, navel and leg by uttering the *bījamantra* consisting of five syllabic words such as *hrāṁ*, *hrīṁ*, *hruṁ*, *hrauṁ*, *hraḥ* respectively. The deities, who are placed on the head, the face, the heart, the navel and the legs, are collectively known as the *pañcaparameṣṭhī* or the five perfect beings.[2] In the *Jvālinī-Kalpa*, Malliṣena emphasizes the necessity of observing the rite of *sakalīkaraṇa* without which it is impossible to attain success in the rites relating to *stambhana*.[3] It refers first to the *nyāsa* of the fingers of the right hand by uttering the mystic words such as *vaṁ*, *maṁ*, *haṁ*, *saṁ* and *taṁ*.[4] It is followed by the *nyāsa* of the left hand reciting another *bījamantra*.[5] So, there are different mystic formulas for performing the *nyāsa* of the different parts of the body.

The *Jvālinī-Kalpa* contains description of no less than a score of *maṇḍalas* or magic circles, which played a prominent role in the tantric form of worship. The magic circle, which contains the mystic figures of gods and goddesses, is used as a vantage ground to summon the evil spirits. Chapter 4 of the *Jvālinī-Kalpa* refers to the use of magic circle for averting the influence of *bhūtas* or mischievous spirits,[6] who caused injury to men and destroyed them mysteriously. The magical rite, which is suggested here, is performed in different stages. In the first stage, the worshipper is asked to draw a round circle on plain ground either on the border of a town or in the centre of a village.[7] The circle, which is to be drawn, should measure eight cubits and should be adorned with flags,

1. *Bhairava-Padmāvatī-Kalpa*, ch. 2, pp. 4-8.
2. Ibid. vv. 2-4, p. 4.
3. *Jvālinī-Kalpa*, ch. 3, v. 1, p. 6.
4. Ibid. v. 2.
5. Ibid. v. 3.
6. Ibid. ch. 4, v. 1, p, 13,
7. Ibid.

mirrors, bells, etc.[1] He is then advised to place four pitchers filled with water on the four corners of the diagram. In the third stage, he should draw the figures of *dikpālas* or the guardian deities of different directions. This being done, the worshipper should finally represent the *bhūta* in the centre of the circle, and worship him with flowers, perfumes, and unbroken rice by muttering the special *mantra* prescribed for the goddess Jvālinī.

The above analysis of the Jaina texts on tantrism clearly illustrates the introduction of tantric elements into the worship of the Jaina goddesses in Karnataka. As in the case of Buddhism and Brāhmaṇical religion, tantrism vitally affected Jainism too and influenced the religious outlook of the Karnataka Jaina teachers, who sought the aid of the goddesses for the attainment of ordinary worldly gains and spiritual salvation.

1. *Jvālinī-Kalpa*, v. 2ff, p. 13.

CHAPTER IV

RELIGIOUS RITUALS AND PRACTICES OF THE KARNATAKA JAINAS

Rituals and practices of the Jainas are as simple as their moral code of conduct. They aim at salvation in accordance with the doctrines of Jainism. Some of these are concerned with the ceremony of image worship,[1] and others with the daily and periodical observances of the Jaina monks as well as the laymen. They are designed to serve as aids to spiritual progress and lead the Jainas from the realm of ignorance to the attainment of final liberation.

One of the important Digambara Jaina practices is the *sallekhanā* or voluntary self-sacrifice of life by abandoning food and drink. According to it, an aspirant devotee lies in some holy place and ceases to take food and drink until he meets his death. Thus it may be defined as the voluntary end of life with the object of attaining salvation.

Death by fasting was given a high-place in the Jaina canons. They frankly recommended voluntary self-sacrifice of the body by fasting. The *Uttarādhyayana*[2] refers to wise man's death according to which a person embraces it willingly. It also speaks of the death of an ignorant man who is not willing and prepared to meet his death. The famous Digambara authority, Sāmantabhadra, who flourished during the early years of the Christian era, states in his *Ratnakaraṇḍa-Śrāvakācāra* that if a person gives up his body in unavoidable calamities, famines, extreme old age and incurable disease, with a view to acquiring religious merit, it is known as *sallekhanā*.[3] Somadeva, who flourished in Karnataka in the 10th century, gives a similar account of this ritual. He states that when the body is about to perish like a dry leaf of a lamp without oil, the

1. Jaina rituals relating to image worship have been discussed in Chapter III.
2. *Uttarādhyayanasūtra*, 5, 2-3; SBE, XIV, p. 21.
3. C.R. Jain (tr.), *Ratnakaraṇḍa-Śrāvakācāra*, v. 122, p. 58.

Jainas observe *sallekhanā*.[1] Somadeva also corroborates Sāmantabhadra in other respects. He, for instance, states that one should give up affection for friends, infatuation with riches and illwill towards enemies.[2] He then advises the gradual abandonment of solid food and drinks including water and asks the devotee to concentrate his mind on the *pañcaparameṣṭhī* or a group of five purified graded souls.[3] The desire to live longer, the desire for speedy death, longing for friends, recollection of past happiness and desire for happiness in the next life are the factors which destroy the efficacy of *sallekhanā*.[4] These details suggest that the rite requires spiritual discipline of the mind cultivated over a long period and is to be observed in several phases. In the first phase, the sacrificer selects a solitary place away from living beings. Secondly, he abstains from solid food and takes only liquid. Thirdly, he gives up liquid and takes only pure and warm water. In the fourth stage, he abandons even warm water and observes complete fast till his death. By observing these phases of the *sallekhanā* rite, the devotee frees himself from rebirth. The performance of this rite, therefore, signifies the victory of the soul over the body. Desai[5] aptly considers it as "the practical demonstration of the cardinal tenet of Jaina philosophy, which stresses the supremacy of the human soul."

The Jaina scriptures recommend three procedures for the performance of the *sallekhanā*. The *Ācārāṅgasūtra* mentions (i) *bhaktapratyākhyāna*, (ii) *iṅgita-maraṇa* ; and (iii) *pādapogamana*.[6] According to the first procedure, the sacrificer selects some holy and solitary place. Then he spreads the bed of straw over it, and by giving up food and drink, he puts up bravely with all the physical troubles. He is not allowed to move his limbs under any circumstances. According to the second, he lies down on a bare piece of ground. He is permitted to move his limbs and to walk when he is tired of lying, sitting and

1. *Yaśastilaka*, pt. ii, BK, viii, p. 413, cited in K K. Handiqui, op. cit., p. 287.
2. Cf. *Ratnakaraṇḍa-Śrāvakācāra*, v. 124, p. 60.
3. Ibid. v. 127. p. 60.
4. Ibid. v. 129, p. 61.
5. *JKU*, vi, (1970), pp. 1-6.
6. *Ācārāṅgasūtra*, 7; 1-25, SBE, xxii, pp. 75ff.

standing. But he does all these things without taking food. The third procedure is more difficult than the preceding two methods, and requires the devotee to stand motionless like a tree without taking food and drink till his death. He neither takes care of his body nor takes help from other fellow ascetics.

The prevalence of these three methods for the performance of this vow is well illustrated in most Digambara texts during the period under review. The *Varāṅgacarita*[1] refers to the observance of the third method. But Jinasena in his *Ādipurāṇa* clearly enumerates all these three methods.[2] He adds that the Jaina devotees approached a Jaina teacher, known as the *niryāpakācārya*,[3] who is said to have decided the course, method, etc. of the *sallekhanā* rite. The subjugation of human passions and gradual abandonment of food and drink appeared to be a common feature of all these methods, but the sacrificer could move his body only in one case.

The correct observance of this vow in accordance with the prescribed rules is indicated by epigraphic evidence. A Śravaṇa-Beḷgoḷa epigraph of 700 states that Māsena correctly observed the vow in consonance with the rules of monastic order.[4] The sage Vṛṣabhanandi is reported to have followed for long the path of the conduct before he undertook this vow.[5] Emphasis on the abandonment of food and drink is also referred to in more than one epigraph. Śāntisenamuni, for instance, is said to have given up food and other things on the mountain Beḷgoḷa.[6] In the 10th century, Nemicandra is recorded to have abstained from food for two months and accomplished *samādhi*.[7] Guṇanandi-Karmmaprakṛti-bhaṭāra gave up food for thirty-one days and died by performing this vow.[8]

1. *Varāṅgacarita*, ch. 31, v. 59, p. 306; Also see *Harivaṁśapurāṇa*, pt. ii, ch. 34, vv. 41-2, p. 434.
2. *Ādipurāṇa*, pt. i. ch, 5, vv. 234-5, p. 114.
3. Ibid. v. 231, p. 114.
4. *EC*, ii, SB 27, p. 6.
5. Ibid. SB 75, p. 40.
6. Ibid. SB. 31, p. 7; SB 11, p. 4.
7. *MAR*, 1914, p. 38.
8. *EC*, iv, ch. 51, p. 6.

Inscriptions also refer to the futility of worldly life and certainty of death. A record states that Mahādeva performed this rite realizing the certainty of death.[1] In 1120 Demavatī, at the close of her life, fixed her mind on the *Arhat* or Jina according to the prescribed rites and attained heaven.[2] In 1130 Hoysaḷa seṭṭi, knowing that his end was near, took leave of his relatives and ended his life with a peaceful mind.[3] There are similar other epigraphs, which enlighten us about the right method of observances of this Jaina vow in the 12th century. In 1120 Pocikabbe, mother of the general Gaṅga Rāja, faithfully observed the rule of lying on one side only and performed *sallekhanā* after uttering the Jaina hymns.[4] One year later Lakkale or Lakṣmīmatī, the wife of the above Jaina general adopted *sanyāsana* and ended her life by *samādhi*.[5]

There are different technical terms for denoting this mode of death. The term *sallekhanā* is used in a few epigraphs Most epigraphs use two other terms (i) *samādhi*[6] and (ii) *sanyāsana*.[7] Apart from these technical terms, the epigraphs also use the expression, "having observed the vow, attained perfection or happiness or became a participator in the happiness of the world of gods." The *Varāṅgacarita* refers to the term *paṇḍitamṛtyu*[8] to indicate the ritual of fasting up to death.

On the basis of the famous Bhadrabāhu-Candragupta Jaina tradition, mentioned in an inscription of the 7th century, the origin of this rite may be traced as far back as the 4th century B.C. It narrates that Bhadrabāhu, who predicted a twelve-year famine in the North, went to Śravaṇa-

1. *EC*. ii, SB 80, p. 41; SB 106, p. 44.
2. Ibid. SB 129, pp. 56-7.
3. Ibid. SB 159, p. 78.
4. Ibid. SB 118, pp. 48-9.
5. Ibid. SB 128, p. 56.
6. *EC*, ii, SB 1, 2, 22, 23, 59, 93, 95, 106, 108, 114, 129, etc. *MAR*, 1914, no. 63, p. 38.
7. Ibid. SB 15, 24-25, 33-34, 75-77, 88, 97, 102, etc. *EC*, ix, cp. 70, p. 145; Ibid. Br, 94, p. 19.
8. *Varāṅgacarita*, ch. 31, v. 59, p. 306.

Beḷgoḷa in Mysore, accompanied by his chief disciple Candragupta Maurya. On reaching Śravaṇa-Beḷgoḷa, he ordered the Jaina community to proceed on their journey, while he himself stayed on at Candragiri hill. He died there by the Jaina rite of fasting. Upon the death of Bhadrabāhu, Candragupta continued there as an ascetic for several years worshipping the footprints of his guru (teacher) till his death by the Jaina rite of *sallekhanā*. This tradition, which has not been questioned by Jaina scholars, does not stand on solid ground on account of the lack of definite proof. We have no contemporary literary and epigraphic evidence to support this Jaina tradition. But there is no doubt that the practice of *sallekhanā* prevailed among the Karnataka Jainas from the 7th century.

By the 8th century, the ritual became very popular in Karnataka. We have only five cases[1] of death by fasting in the 7th century, but there are about fifty-four cases recorded in the 8th century. Of the fifty four cases mentioned above, forty three[2] refer to men, mostly monks, and ten[3] commemorate the death of nuns. Inscriptions dealing with the subject reveal two categories of monks, spiritual teachers who were called *ācārya*, *bhaṭṭāraka* and *sūri*, and the ordinary monks who were not given any title of respect. The nuns also accepted this mode of death as bravely as the monks. They did not lag behind the monks in religious austerities and exhibited the same tenacity in observing *sallekhanā*.

The Karnataka Jainas continued to perform this ritual vigorously during the 10th-12th centuries. Inscriptions show that this rite prevailed not only among the monks and nuns but also among the Jaina laity. Some epigraphs from Śravaṇa-Beḷgoḷa speak of its observance by men and women of high social status. Indra IV, for instance, is recorded to have died in the typical Jaina fashion of *sallekhanā* at Śravaṇa-Beḷgoḷa in the 10th century.[4] Similarly the Gaṅga king Mārasiṁha is

1. *EC*, ii, SB 1, 650 A.D., p. 1; SB 2, 650 A.D., p. 2; SB 11, 650 A.D., p. 4; SB 31, 650 A.D., p. 7; SB 75, 650 A.D., p. 40.
2. Cf. Appendix—'B', nos. 1 to 44.
3. Cf. Appendix—'B', nos. 45 to 54.
4. *EC*, ii, SB 133, 982 A.D., pp. 61-3; ibid. xii, SB 27, p. 92.

said to have accomplished *samādhi* in the presence of Ajitasena-bhaṭṭāraka at Bankapur in the district of Dharwar.[1] Their ministers and feudatories also followed this ritual. An inscription of the same century informs us that Nāgavarma, the son-in-law of Narasinga, who served the Gaṅga king Ereganga as minister renounced this world and observed this Jaina vow.[2] Another inscription records the death of Kiviriyya who kept the vow for twelve days in the Cangalva *basadi* and expired.[3]

The royal ladies of Karnataka did not fail to observe this rite. Pāmbabbe, a very austere Jaina lady, who was the elder sister of the Gaṅga king Būtuga, died by fasting in 971.[4] Another such royal lady was Pullapa, the younger sister of Cāmuṇḍarāya, the famous minister of the Gaṅga king Mārasiṁha. A *niṣidhi* (called here *niṣidikā* of Pullapa) was set up to commemorate this event.[5] Moreover, Jakkiyabbe, who served as the governor of Nagarakhaṇḍa 70 under the Rāṣṭrakūṭas, performed this rite at the holy place called Bandanike in full faith.[6] There is similar other epigraphic evidence to show the impact of this Jaina vow on the princess of Mysore during the 11th-12th centuries. Pocikabbe,[7] Śāntaladevī[8], Macikabbe[9], Boppave[10], and Lakṣmīmatī[11] were such royal patronesses who ended their lives by observing the Jaina vow of self-sacrifice. These examples clearly prove that Jainism had made a deep impression on the minds of the people of royal families. Although men and women of royal houses were accustomed to a life of comfort and luxury, they were prepared to undergo severe austerities involved in the vow of *sallekhanā*.

1. *EC*, ii, SB 59, 974 A.D., p. 14; *EI*, v, no. 18, p. 180.
2. Ibid. SB 150, 950 A.D., p. 76.
3. Ibid. i, Cg. 30, 1050 A.D., p. 64.
4. Ibid. vi, kd. 1, p. 1.
5. *Top. List of Insc.*, no. 597 of 1905, i, p. 545.
6. *EC*, vii, Sk. 219, pp. 230-1.
7. *EC*, ii, SB 118, pp. 48-9.
8. B.A. Saletore, op. cit., p. 166.
9. *EC*, ii, SB 140, pp. 65-7.
10. Ibid. viii, Tr. 198, p. 207.
11. Ibid. ii, SB 127-8, pp. 51-6.

The ritual also prevailed among the lower strata of the Jaina society. This is corroborated by the evidence of an epigraph from Śravaṇa-Beḷgoḷa. It refers to two lay devotees, Ereyapa-gāvuṇḍa and Maddaya, who are said to have died by the orthodox Jaina rite in the 10th century.[1] Another record speaks of the death of Bīliya-seṭṭi, lying down with devotion at the feet of the Jaina ascetic in the 11th century.[2] In the 12th century, Hoysaḷa-Seṭṭi, taking leave of his relatives, ended his life with a peaceful mind.[3] Another record of 1139[4] reports the death of Singimayya by the rite of *samādhi* at Śravaṇa-Beḷgoḷa. Thus it can be safely stated that the practice of *sallekhanā* was prevalent among all classes of the Karnataka Jainas in the early medieval period.

In a few cases, the period of fast is mentioned. Fasting for the duration of three days,[5] twelve-days,[6] twenty one days,[7] one month[8] and two months[9] are referred to in some epigraphs. Fasting for the duration of three days is referred to in an epigraph of the 10th century, although it is difficult to believe that three days' fasting can bring death to a man. Possibly, the sacrificer had given up food even before entering the period of this ritual. He tried to reduce the period of *sallekhanā* to the minimum to avoid the disturbances caused by his relatives. But the reduction of the period of this rite was only possible in the case of laymen. This is clearly illustrated by the evidence of the above-mentioned record. It commemorates the death of the Gaṅga King Mārasiṁha at Bankapur in the district of Dharwar.

Most epigraphs refer to Candragiri hill at Śravaṇa-Beḷgoḷa in the Hassan district as the most sacred place for

1. *EC*, ii, SB 468, p. 87.
2. Ibid. i, Cg. 30, p. 64.
3. Ibid. ii, SB 159, p. 78.
4. Ibid. SB 142, pp. 69-70.
5. Ibid. SB 59, p. 14.
6. Ibid. i, Cg. 30, p. 64.
7. Ibid. ii, SB 33, p. 7.
8. Ibid. SB 25, p. 6; ibid. SB 143, p. 73.
9. *MAR*, 1914, p. 38.

performing this rite. It appears that the Jainas tried to choose a place which was supposed to be peaceful and free from living beings. On account of difficult access, the mountain formed a natural barrier between the sacrificer and his near relatives. This is why they preferred to die on the summit of the mountain. The Śravaṇa-Beḷgoḷa epigraphs show that people from distant places came to spend their last days there during the 7th-9th centuries. But in later times, we notice some change in the selection of the place for performing this rite. The Jainas appeared to have observed this vow in the Jaina temples. It is corroborated by some epigraphs belonging to the 10th century. Bandanike in the Shimoga district and Bankapura in the Dharwar district and Kopaṇa or modern Kopbal in Raichur district developed as the Jaina tīrthas (places of pilgrimage) for performing this ritual during the 10th-12th centuries. It was the natural outcome of the Jaina practice which led to the foundation of innumerable Jaina temples in Karnataka during early medieval times.

It will not be fair to charge the Jainas with the guilt of committing suicide as it has been done by the non-Jainas. Pūjyapāda states that it cannot be called suicide because the Jaina observes it willingly at the end of his life with pleasure. It cannot be forced upon anyone.[1] As there is no attachment to worldly objects, no desire and no passion in this undertaking, the devotee cannot be regarded to have committed suicide. The *Varāṅgacarita* condemns[2] the practice of suicide and forbids the Jaina devotees to accept this mode of death. It states clearly that suicide by hanging, by entering fire, by falling into the water, by taking poison, by striking with sharp weapons, etc., are not permitted by the Jaina sages. In fact, the Jainas performed this rite, when physical disability made them unable to advance their spiritual career for the attainment of liberation. As life became a drag and hindrance to the pursuit of self-purification, it naturally lost its significance. Thus, the Jainas wisely abandoned their lives by performing this ritual of self-sacrifice.

1. *Sarvārtha siddhi*, sh. 7, v. 22, p. 362.
2. *Varāṅgacarita*, ch. 15, vv. 65ff, pp. 133-4.

The Jaina practice of *sallekhanā* also differed greatly from the Brāhmaṇical practice of observing religious suicide. While the Jainas observed it voluntarily, the Hindu practice of religious suicide was involuntary. The ritual suicide of a Jaina woman cannot be regarded as a substitute for *sati* as it has been done by a scholar.[1] The wives of the Jainas were not accustomed to follow their husbands after death just as it was prevalent among the Hindu women. Secondly, the practice of *sati* was observed even against the will of the widow woman, but the Jaina vow of *sallekhanā* could not be forced upon her under any circumstances. A few epigraphs of the 10th century show that the Jaina widow Jakkiyabbe rendered valuable service to society after the death of her husband. She decided to observe this vow only when she was afflicted with old age and physical infirmity.[2] That *sallekanā* was not a custom parallel to *sati* is indicated by the fact that the Jaina women died by this mode of death even though their husbands were alive. Lakṣmīmatī is said to have ended her life by observing this vow and her husband erected an epitaph at Śravaṇa-Beḷgoḷa to perpetuate her memory.[3]

Jaina Initiation Rite

The initiation ritual of the Jainas figures frequently in the Karnataka Jaina texts as the most important rite. It marks the end of worldly life and takes the Jaina to the door of asceticism, inspired by the high ideal of attaining spiritual liberation. Thus, a Jaina enters the monastic order for his spiritual uplift just as a student enters an academic institution for his intellectual proficiency.

The process of initiation and prescribed rules for the performance of this ceremony persist with slight alterations during early medieval times. The novice, who wants to renounce the world, is advised first to seek the permission of his elders and relatives for initiation.[4] He is not advised to disobey

1. S.R. Sharma, op. cit., p. 164.
2. *EC*, vii, SK. 219, pp. 130-1.
3. Ibid. ii, SB. 128, p. 56.
4. *Padmapurāṇa*, pt. i, ch. 3, v. 282, p. 52; ibid. ch. 5, v. 68, p. 72; *Harivaṁśapurāṇa*, pt. ii, ch. 34, v. 31, p. 433.

them under any circumstances, as is evident from the *Varāṅga-carita*. Prince Varāṅga renounces the world only when he takes the consent of his father.[1] Taking leave of his relatives, he approaches a Digambara *ācārya* and prostrates himself before him with a view to showing respect. He then expresses his desire for initiation. When he obtains his approbation, the day of initiation is fixed with the help of a *śrāvaka* (layman) who has expert knowledge of astrology, incantations, omens and unseen things.[2] Jinasena also states that the aspiring candidate for attaining emancipation should be initiated into the monastic order on the auspicious day and moment. He prohibits the initiation of a novice on the day of lunar eclipse, dark-cloud day and during the leap-year.[3] He adds further that if an *ācārya* (teacher) does not initiate a novice at the appropriate moment, he should be expelled from the Jaina monastic order.[4] This shows that astrological consideration influenced the Jaina rites.

Another element in the Jaina initiation, for which there is confirmation in all the Digambara texts, is the extraction of hair by the roots.[5] The novice uprooted his hair from his head and beard with his own hand. It was repeated at the interval of two, three and four months. The extraction of hair at the interval of every two months was deemed as the ideal period for it. The Jaina practice of uprooting the hair was undoubtedly an ordeal, intended to test the firm resolution of the novice. It also exhibited non-attachment towards the body and protection of the Jaina vow of *ahiṁsā* or non-injury. An analogous practice of uprooting the hair is to be met with among the Ājīvika ascetics who also pull out their hair with a piece of the rib of a palm leaf.[6] We have epigraphic evidence to show the prevalence of this practice among the Karnataka

1. *Varāṅgacarita*, ch. 29, vv. 9ff, pp. 284ff.
2. K.K. Handiqui, op. cit., p. 284.
3. *Ādipurāṇa*, pt. ii, ch. 39, v. 157, p. 283.
4. Ibid. v. 161, p. 284.
5. *Varāṅgacarita*, ch. 30, v. 2, p. 293; *Harivaṁśapurāṇa*, pt. i, ch. 2, v. 52, p. 16.
6. A.L. Basham, *History and Doctrines of the Ājīvikas*, p. 106.

Jainas. An epigraph of the 10th century[1] speaks of Pāmbabbe, the elder sister of the Gaṅga king Būtuga, who is said to have made her head bald and performed penance for thirty years for the attainment of spiritual liberation.

In the next stage, the novice gives up his entire clothings and costly ornaments and assumes the form of a new born child.[2] It is an essential Jaina rite for a Digambara monk who is enjoined to observe the Jaina vow of *aparigraha* or non-possesssion. Hence, even the later Jaina writers have advocated the Jaina practice of nudity. Somadeva insists[3] on its observance because nakedness is natural. He states further that it is impossible for a Digambara monk to observe the vow of non-possession if he desires to wear robes made of barks and deer-skins.[4] Thus, the Karnataka Jaina texts mention a number of kings, princes, ministers and merchants who gave up their costly clothings and ornaments and became naked at the time of initiation.

After performing all these essential rites, the *ācārya* (teacher) initiates him into the monastic order by giving him the lesson of *pañcaparameṣṭhīmantra*.[5] It is followed by the *nāmakaraṇa* rite (naming of monks), according to which the entrant is given entirely a new name. Pūjyapāda is said to have been named as Devanandi after initiation in the Śravaṇa-Belgoḷa epigraphs.[6] Lastly, the ācārya instructs him in the essential duties of a monk. The initiation deprives him of bath and teeth cleaning.

The novice undergoes a rigorous course of training after initiation into the order. The preceptor prepares him for right conduct by teaching him the rules of the monastic discipline. If he fails to develop his strength in the practice of monastic discipline under one preceptor, he is transferred to another

1. *EC*, vi, Kd. 1, p. 1.
2. *Varāṅgacarita*, ch. 29, vv. 86-7, p. 291; *Harivaṁśapurāṇa*, pt. i, ch. 2, v. 69, p. 17; *Ādipurāṇa*, pt. ii, ch. 39, v. 160, p. 254.
3. *Yaśastilaka*, pt. ii, BK. 6, p. 281.
4. K.K. Handiqui, op. cit., p. 253.
5. *Ādipurāṇa*, pt. ii, ch. 39, v. 43, p. 272.
6. *JSB*, pt. v, no. 1, (June 1938), p. 1.

instructor. Jinasena Sūri in his *Harivaṁśapurāṇa* refers to a newly initiated monk who learns the proper conduct under three instructors in a year and a half.[1] After the completion of the probation period, he becomes a qualified member of the monastic order. Emphasis on the correct observance of the rules of initiation also figures in a record of 1169 in which Śrīpāla-traividya is said to have maintained the proper rules of *dīkṣā* (initiation) and *śikṣā* (instruction) in the 12th century.[2]

The initiation ceremony of a nun did not differ much from that of a monk except in regard to the observance of nudity. In other words, a monk was bound to go naked at the time of initiation, which was not permissible in the case of a nun. It may mean the preservation of the traditional status of women folk according to Hindu mythology. However, such a practice on the occasion of initiation ceremony was not at all entertained in Buddhism. The *Varāṅgacarita* states that several queens of Varāṅga renounced the world and took to a life of a nun. They did obeisance to their preceptors and went to a lonely place where they discarded their ornaments and retained only pure white *sārī* (lower garment for women) in order to cover nudity. They also pulled out their hair.[3] The literary evidence regarding the initiation of Jaina ladies is corroborated by an epigraph from Śravaṇa-Beḷgoḷa. It informs us that Macikabbe and Śāntikabbe received suitable initiation from the Jaina teacher Bhānukīrti in the 12th century.[4]

The Jaina initiation was a gradual preparation for the adoption of an ascetic life. The *Ratnakaraṇḍa-Śrāvakācāra* divided the life of a householder into eleven stages. As he has to pass through these successive stages before entering the monastic order, he is supposed to learn right conduct of a house-holder for a number of years. So, the old age was generally considered fit for initiation.

1. *Harivaṁśapurāṇa*, pt. ii, ch. 33, v. 71ff., p. 422.
2. *EC*, v, AK 1, pp. 112-3.
3. *Varāṅgacarita*, ch. 29, vv. 93-4, p. 292.
4. *EC*, ii, SB 137, p. 64.

But the Jaina teachers of Karnataka did not insist on advanced age for renunciation during early medieval times. They frankly recommended all ages for taking initiation. Ravisena advocates renunciation even during childhood. As death spares none, the consideration of age is held insignificant.[1] The *Yaśastilaka* also refers to Abhayaruci and Abhayamati, the twin disciples of the sage Sudatta, who are said to have renounced the world at a fairly young age. As old age raises obstacles in the path of liberation because of physical infirmity, Prince Varāṅga points out the necessity of taking initiation at the young age with a view to practising the severe Jaina austerities.[2]

The Digambaras in Karnataka provide almost the same list of persons unfit for initiation[3] as the Śvetāmbaras do. But the exclusion of the Śūdras from entering the monastic order appears to be the chief feature of Karnataka Jainism in the early medieval period. Since the beginning of the 9th century there is evidence to show that the Śūdras are excluded from religious initiation. Jinasena in his *Ādipurāṇa* states that a person whose ancestral lineage is pure, who bears a good conduct, and is not devoid of physical deficiency is entitled to initiation into monkhood.[4] Somadeva makes it more clear by stating that only three higher castes, i.e., *brāhmaṇa*, kṣatriya and vaiśya are eligible for religious initiation.[5] It is apparently a deviation from the original teachings of Jainism which vehemently condemns the caste system during the early years of its foundation. Jainism was now infected by the Hindu varṇa system, and hence caste spirit soon reasserted its power within the Jaina religion in Karnataka during early medieval times.

The consideration of caste and creed for religious initiation of the Jainas clearly indicates the organisation of the Jaina community on the basis of varṇa scheme of the Hindus. It is evident from the study of the *Padmapurāṇa* of Ravisena

1. *Padmapurāṇa*, pt. ii, ch. 31, vv. 132-3, p. 76.
2. *Varāṅgacarita*, ch. 29, vv. 12ff, p. 284.
3. Cf. C.R. Jain, *Sannyāsa-dharma*, pp. 23ff.
4. *Ādipurāṇa*, pt. ii, ch. 39, v. 158, p. 283.
5. *Yaśastilaka*, pt. ii, BK. viii, p. 405.

who gives the Jaina version of the creation of the varṇa organisation[1] and tells us how Ṛṣabhadeva created the four varṇas from different parts of his body. Jinasena[2] also repeats the same idea in his *Ādipurāṇa*. He clearly shows that each of the four varṇas performed their duties assigned to them. Thus, the Jainas became strong supporters of caste system like their brāhmaṇical counterparts. The prevalence of the fourfold Aryan division of society, which was accepted by the Jainas of Karnataka, indicates the influence of Aryan ideas and institutions over the masses of Dravidian populations.[3]

We notice another important change in the outlook of the Jaina teachers who initiated a novice into the monastic order. Probably they charged some fees for initiation. An epigraph of the 8th century[4] refers to the initiation of a person named Singam and tells us that his mother Aratti made a grant of land probably as a reward for performing this rite. Another epigraph from Śravaṇa-Beḷgoḷa informs us that Bhānukīrti of the Mūlasaṅgha was rewarded for initiating Macikabbe and Śāntikabbe. Both these ladies entered the monastic order in 1137 and built a beautiful Jaina temple, which was endowed with rich gifts for the performance of Jina worship and for providing food to the ascetics. Thus, the monetary consideration seems to have influenced the Jaina rite of initiation in Karnataka.

Domestic Rituals of the Karnataka Jainas

Jinasena is the first to furnish an exhaustive list of domestic rites for the Jainas of Karnataka during the early medieval period. Although in the *Ādipurāṇa* he refers to fifty-three rites prescribed for the whole life of the Jaina laity from conception to the attainment of liberation, only twenty-two of these rites are concerned with the domestic rituals of the Karnataka Jainas. The list of twenty two rites is as follows :

Ādhāna or *garbhādhāna* is a rite to be observed to obtain a

1. *Padmapurāṇa*, pt. i, ch. 4, vv. 86 ff, p. 63-64.
2. *Ādipurāṇa*, pt. i, ch, 16, vv. 243f, p. 368.
3. S.R. Sharma, op. cit., p. 156.
4. *EC*, iii, My. 25, p. 3.

male offspring. Jinasena advises the Jainas to worship the Jina with proper recitation of Jaina mantra on the occasion of performing this ritual. They are then advised to offer oblation to the three sacred fires, as was done on the occasion of attaining salvation by the Jainas. After observing the preceding rites, the couple is allowed to unite for obtaining a son.[1]

Prīti is a Jaina rite to preserve the pregnancy of a woman in the third month, which is performed by the Jaina Brāhmaṇas in the Jaina temple. Jinasena prescribes the erection of an arch (*toraṇa*) and establishment of two water vessels on each side of the door of the householder's house. Jinasena also lays down rules for making provisions for playing of drums and the sounding of bells on this pious occasion according to the economic capacity of the Jainas.[2]

Jinasena then refers to two important rites, which are termed as the *supriti* and the *dhṛti* rite for the prosperity and welfare of the pregnant woman. He ordains the Jainas to perform the former rite in the presence of the sacred fires kindled before the Jina image with the proper recitation of Jaina hymns in the fifth month from her conception[3] and to observe the latter in the seventh month of the pregnancy, preceded by the worship of the Jina.[4]

The next puberty rite is termed as the *moda* for the fullest completion of the woman's pregnancy in the 9th month. The woman is decked with ornaments and costly clothings. Then, a girdle, called *gātrika-bandha* containing the Jaina hymns is tied around her waist for the protection of the foetus. The rite is performed by the Jaina Brāhmaṇas before the image of the Jina.[5] The *priyodbhava* or *Jātakarma* rite is performed on the occasion of the birth of the child. Jinasena advises the Jainas to observe this rite carefully after reciting the Jaina hymns before the Jina.[6]

1. *Ādipurāṇa*, pt. ii, ch. 38, vv. 70-6, p. 245.
2. Ibid. vv. 77-9, p. 246.
3. Ibid. vv. 80-1, p. 246.
4. Ibid. v. 82, p. 246.
5. Ibid. vv. 83-4, p. 246.
6. Ibid. pt. ii, ch. 38, vv. 85-6, p. 246.

The *nāmakaraṇa* or rite of naming the boy is performed after the twelfth day of his birth on an auspicious day, which suits well his parents. The Jainas worship the Jina and pay homage to the Jaina ascetics on this occasion. The name of the boy is selected from the one thousand and eight names of Jinendra through the process of *ghaṭapatra* method. The Jainas are advised to write the names of the Jinas on separate pieces of papers which are stored and mixed in an earthen pot. Then, a boy is asked to take out a piece of paper from the pot. The boy is named after the name of the Jina which is taken out of the lot.[1]

The *bahiryāna* or the rite of taking the child out of the house is performed in the second, third or fourth month after his birth. The Jainas, according to Jinasena, should make arrangements for the playing of musical instruments on this occasion. Gifts should be presented to the boy by his parents and relatives. Presents should be preserved, and finally handed over to the boy when he is mature enough to inherit his ancestral property.[2] The boy has to be placed on some sacred seat (*āsana*) in order to increase his ability for attaining temporal and spiritual position. The householders are enjoined to repeat the same process of the Jina worship on this occasion.[3]

When the boy is seven or eight months old, the rite of feeding him is observed, according to which cooked food is offered to him for the first time. Jinasena calls it as the *annaprāśana* Jaina rite.[4] The *varṣavardhana* or birth anniversary is perfomed when the boy becomes one-year old. Jinasena advises the Jainas to celebrate it every year. They are further ordained to bestow gifts and feed the elders and near relatives.[5]

In the *caula* or *cūḍākarma* rite, the head of the boy is shaved with a razor on an auspicious day and a lock of hair is left in the middle of his head. When the boy is bathed in pure water and dressed well, he is asked to offer obeisance to the Jina

1. *Ādipurāṇa*, pt. ii, ch. 38, vv. 87-9, p. 247.
2. Ibid. vv. 90-2, p. 247.
3. Ibid. vv. 93-4, p. 247.
4. Ibid. 95, p. 248.
5. Ibid. vv. 96-7, p. 248.

and the Jaina ascetics. The rite ends when the boy receives blessings from his parents.[1] In the fifth year the Jaina boy has to perform the *lipisaṅkhāyana* rite or the rite of learning the alphabet. He is handed over to some Jaina preceptor, appointed by his parents for proper training.[2]

The *Upaniti* rite or the practice of wearing sacred thread, which is not a Jaina custom, became popular in early medieval times. Jinasena in his *Ādipurāṇa* enlightens us for the first time about it and enjoins all the householders to use the sacred thread .

The rite is performed when the boy becomes eight years old. It is preceded by the rite of tonsure ceremony and acceptance of the five lesser Jaina vows, meant for the Jaina householders only. The boy is asked to worship the Jina in the Jaina temples. Afterwards, a rope of *muñjā-grass,* consisting of three threads, is tied round his waist by the Jaina Brāhmaṇas.[3] They symbolize the three Jaina jewels of good learning, good knowledge and good conduct. The boy then puts on white lower garment, and as a symbol of the Jaina vows, he is invested with the sacred thread. Lastly, Jinasena prescribes the begging of alms[4] for subsistence of the boy. Whatever he brings from begging is first offered to the Jina and the remainder is consumed by the boy. Jinasena puts restrictions on the movement of the royal princes, who, unlike the Jaina commoners, are enjoined to beg food within the palace premises. Such restrictions are not prescribed for the common people adhering to the Jaina faith. It appears that Jinasena makes social distinctions in the observance of the Jaina rituals and has safeguarded the interest of aristocratic class in Karnataka.

But the use of sacred thread was not received by the Jaina puritans of Gujarat and other places of the North even after the composition of *Ādipurāṇa* in the 9th century.[5] The

1. *Ādipurāṇa*, pt. ii. ch. 38, vv.98-101, p. 248.
2. Ibid. vv. 102-3, p. 248.
3. Ibid. vv. 104-12, p. 249.
4. Ibid. vv. 107-8, p. 249.
5. N.R. Premi, op. cit., p. 508.

Śvetāmbaras also did not make provision for the sacred thread ceremony.[1]

When the boy is invested with the sacred thread, he is expected to lead the life of a celibate. Jinasena advises him to practise *vratacaryā* or the Jaina vows. He is neither allowed to clean his teeth nor taste betel leaf or anything else. He is asked to take bath in pure water and to sleep on bare ground. Then he learns the duties of a layman and takes lessons in grammar, astrology, mathematics, ethics, etc., from the Jaina preceptor.[2]

After the completion of learning, the boy is enjoined to abstain from taking meat, honey, etc., which according to Jaina doctrines, are the breeding ground of various living organisms. This rite is observed in the twelfth year of the boy in the presence of his preceptor before the Jina image.[3]

The boy has to seek the permission of his preceptor for marriage, which is performed after the end of education.[4] After marriage the bridegroom is enjoined to remain celibate for seven days during which he is required to visit the sacred places of Jainism.[5] Then husband and wife are allowed to mate especially during the period of menstruation with the object of getting a son. A weak and infirm Jaina is advised to abstain from sexual intercourse for the prosperity of his health.[6]

The Jainas observe the *varaṇalābha* rite,[7] which establishes them firmly in the household affairs. The son inherits the ancestral wealth in accordance with his father's will. Jainasena ordains the father to worship the Jina and then to hand over his property to his son in the presence of eminent Jaina householders in the Jaina temple. The father instructs his son to practise the conduct befitting a layman

1. N. R. Premi, op. cit. p. 509.
2. *Ādipurāṇa*, pt. ii, ch. 38, vv. 112-20, pp. 249-50.
3. Ibid. vv. 121-4, p. 250.
4. Ibid. v. 127, p. 251.
5. Ibid . vv. 131-2, p. 251.
6. Ibid. vv. 133-4, p. 251.
7. Ibid. v. 135, p. 251.

and to bestow gifts upon the Jainas for the increment of his wealth and fame.[1] Thus Jinasena endeavours to propagate the Jaina faith even among the offspring of the Jaina householders.

The Jainas are instructed to earn their livelihood by proper means and to practise the six essential Jaina duties,[2] i.e., the worship of the Jina, study of the spiritual lore, control of passions, charity, etc. By following the rules of good conduct, they make themselves able to withstand the Jaina austerities and finally develop dislike for worldly life. In this stage, they are enjoined to observe various fasts so that they can act like the Jaina ascetics and contemplate over the nature of the soul.[3] Jinasena, thus, prescribes the abandonment of the household life. The public declaration of renunciation is to be preceded by the worship of the Jina.

The purposes behind the Jaina domestic rituals are manifold : popular conviction, material profit, cultural and spiritual gains. Like the Hindus, the Jainas believed that by performing the various rites, they may avert the evil influences which overtake pregnant women and children. The Jaina householders are advised to invoke the help of the Jinas to drive out foul influences. Jinasena enjoins that the *gātrika-bandha*, containing Jaina hymns, should be placed over the body of a pregnant woman. This was supposed to protect the foetus during the 9th month of her pregnancy.

The Jaina sacraments were meant for acquiring progeny, long life and wealth. The Jainas believed that prayers and appeals made to the Jinas brought forth children and spiritual happiness in the life after death. The *garbhādhāna* rite was performed to obtain a male offspring. Further it was thought that the personality and character of a Jaina householder are formed by observing such rites as the investiture of the sacred thread, the nuptial rite, etc. Finally, these rites were supposed to reconcile the active worldly life of the Jainas with spiritualism.

1. *Ādipurāṇa*, pt. ii, ch. 38, vv. 138-41, p. 252.
2. Ibid. vv. 142-3, p. 252.
3. Ibid. vv. 148 ff, pp. 252-3.

A close study of the Jaina domestic rituals reveals certain fundamental similarities between Jinasena's *Ādipurāṇa* and the Hindu Dharmaśāstras. The chief object of the Jainas in performing these rites appears to be the same as that found in the Gṛihyasūtras and Smṛtis. According to most Hindu law givers the sacraments are intended to sanctify the body from the moment of conception to the death of a person. This is also the view of Jinasena, who states in his *Ādipurāṇa* that like a precious stone taken out from the mine, the human soul attains perfection through purificatory rites, accompanied by the sacred Jaina mantras.[1]

Jinasena extols the fire cult like the Vedic literature. He justifies the worship of the sacred fire on practical grounds. He states in his *Ādipurāṇa* that fire is neither divine nor holy but it becomes so on account of its association with the worship of the Jinas. He, therefore, asks the Jaina householders to kindle three fires before the Jina and offer oblation to them.[2] Consequently, the Jainas of Karnataka appear to have started the worship of the fire cult just as the Brāhmaṇas did on the occasion of performing the sixteen sacraments. Somadeva also supports this practice by stating that a popular custom can be followed so long as it does not come into conflict with the fundamental principles of Jainism.[3] Probably, the Jaina fire cults were the same as the Vedic fire cults and included the worship of such specific fires as *āhavanīya*, *dakṣināgni* and *gārhapatya* in order to fit in with the Jaina system.[4]

The cult of fire ritual was not only prevalent among the Karnataka Jainas but also among the Jainas of Tamil Nadu. The *Śilapaddikāram*[5] indicates the prevalence of this cult in Tamil land in the early centuries of the Christian era. The term *velvi* is always used to denote fire ritual in Tamil language. Whenever the term *velvi* is used alone, it merely means fire ritual without involving animal sacrifice.[6]

1. *Ādipurāṇa*, pt. ii, ch. 39, v. 90, p. 277.
2. *Ādipurāṇa*, pt. ii, ch. 40, vv. 88-91, p. 301.
3. K.K. Handiqui, op. cit., p. 332.
4. N. R. Premi, op. cit., p. 510.
5. The *Śilapaddikāram*, cited in K. K. Handiqui, op. cit., p. 334.
6. Ibid. p. 333.

The sacred thread rite among the Jainas of Karnataka is also based on the Brāhmaṇical idea. According to the *Ādipurāṇa*, the performance of this rite signifies rebirth of the Jaina householders[1] who are called *dvijas* or twice-born after initiation.

The above details show that Jinasena adapts the ancient traditions of the Hindus and harmonizes them with the practices of the Jaina culture. The main line of Hinduization of the Jaina religion runs through Jinasena, who builds an ambitious fabric of Jaina rites on the basis of the prescribed Hindu *saṁskāras* in the 9th century.[2]

The process of Hinduization of the Jaina religion in Karnataka appeared to have set in before the 9th century. It was caused mainly by the entrance of non-Jainas into the Jaina monastic order. The Digambara texts from Karnataka which were composed during the 7th-8th centuries, witnessed the infiltration of Hindu elements in Jaina religious practices and gave it a place of importance to these religious rites.[3] The *Paumacariya* of Vimala Sūri and the *Padmapurāṇa* of Ravisena give us some hint about the sacred thread ceremony. They refer to the term *suttakaṇṭha*, meaning the thread hanging from the neck.[4] Similarly, the Jaina texts are replete with references to the performance of the Jaina rites of marriage, learning, etc. But it was Jinasena who gave it a final shape in his work *Ādipurāṇa*. He recognized them with a view to championing the cause of Jainism in the South. The appearance of Śaṅkarācārya in the 8th-9th centuries proved detrimental to the existence of the Jainas in the south. He started a systematic campaign against the Jainas and denounced them as atheists and tried to excite people against them. In this situation, the Jaina teachers of Karnataka showed far-sightedness by assimilating Hindu elements for maintaining their position.[5]

Despite the similarities with the Hindu domestic rituals,

1. *Ādipurāṇa*, pt. ii, ch. 40, vv. 158-9, 310.
2. Robert Williams, *Jaina Yoga*, Introd. p. xxii-xiii.
3. *JSB*, pt. vi, no. 4, (March 1940), p. 206.
4. N.R. Premi, op. cit., p. 507.
5. *JSB*, pt. vi, no. 4, (March 1940) p. 206.

the Jainas emphasize *ahiṁsā* (non-injury). Jinasena warns the Jaina householders against the use of meat, honey etc, which are considered unfit for the performance of the Jaina rites on account of their connection with *hiṁsā* (injury).

The imitation of the Hindu sacraments by Jinasena goes against the original teachings of Jainism. The early Jaina boldly protests against Vedic ritualism and the priests presiding over it. But the Jainas of Karnataka observed many Brāhmaṇical rites during the early medieval age. Jinasena gave recognition to the *dvijas*, evidently the Jaina Brāhmaṇas who officiated in the performance of their domestic rites.

Artisans, dancers[1] and probably the śūdras are not allowed to wear the sacred thread. Jinasena forbids them to put on the sacred thread on account of their low birth. He allows them to wear a lower garment called *dhotī*, which is a substitute for the sacred thread. All this shows deviation from early Jainism, which does not recognize social distinctions in religious observances.

Dāna or Charity Ritual

The Jaina literature on *dāna* or charity is enormous. Apart from the casual references to it in the Jaina Purāṇas, Book VIII section 43 of the *Yaśastilaka* is entirely devoted to the various aspects of charity ritual, such as the objects of gift, the qualifications of the donee, and the best method of giving donation. The Jaina teachers of Karnataka extol the virtues of making gifts to the Jaina ascetics, and the sick, infirm and poor persons belonging to the Jaina faith. They consider it to be the most effective means of securing religious merit and attaining liberation.[2] It relieves the donors of sufferings and dangers and brings them worldly happiness both in the present and future life.[3] Jinasena glorifies charity as the most proper way of spending one's wealth or possession.[4]

Regular endowment of gift is considered as one of the

1. *Ādipurāṇa*, pt. ii, ch. 40. vv. 170-1, p. 311.
2. Ibid. pt. i, ch. 16, v. 271, p. 371;
   Paramātmaprakāśa, ch. 2, v. 168, p. 312.
3. *Padmapurāṇa*, pt. iii, ch. 96, vv. 16-7, p. 197.
4. *Ādipurāṇa*, pt. ii, ch. 38, v. 270, p. 264.

six essential duties of the Jaina householders[1], and this is corroborated by a large number of Jaina epigraphs which record gifts either for the Jaina monks or Jaina establishments.

Dāna-śālās or charity houses are often attached to the Jaina *basadis*, as can be shown from the inscriptions of the 7th-8th centuries. In 683, the western Cālukya king Vinayāditya granted the village named Hadagile situated in Beluvala-300 for a dāna-śālā.[2] In 730 Vijayāditya, another king of the same dynasty, donated the village Kaddama to the south of Purikaranagara for the maintenance of a charity house, attached to the Saṅkha-Jinendra temple at modern Lakshmesvara in the district of Dharwar.[3] Five years later, Vikramāditya II granted 50 *nivartanas* of land for meeting the cost of expenditure of almshouse, which was attached to the Dhavala-Jinālaya at the same place.[4] The practice continues in subsequent times. The rich and pious Jainas delighted in making endowments for maintaining charity houses and establishing new ones for advancing the cause of *dāna* or charity. It is substantiated by the donative records of the 10th-12th centuries. An epigraph of the 10th century registers the gift of a tank for the charity house attached to the Jaina temple at Naragel in the district of Dharwar.[5] Another epigraph of the 11th century refers to the donation of some land for the Samyakratnākara *basadi* at Mugad in the district of Dharwar and the income incurred from that land was to be utilised for feeding the visitors.[6] In 1074 the mahāsāmanta Kāṭarsa gave gifts of land for the benefit of the charity house of the Gaṅga-Permāḍi Jaina temple at Aṇṇigere in the Navalgund taluq.[7] The Śāntara kings donated two villages for providing food to the Jaina monks living in the Pañcakūṭa *basadi* in the Nagar taluq of Shimoga district.[8] We have similar

1. *Yaśastilaka*, pt. ii, BK. viii, Section 46, p. 414.
2. *BKI*, iv, no. 4, p. 3.
3. Ibid. no. 6, p.6.
4. Ibid. no. 7, p. 7.
5. Ibid. i, pt. i, no. 38, p. 23.
6. Ibid. no. 78, p. 68.
7. *EI*, xv, no. 23, p. 346.
8. *EC*, viii, Nr. 40, A.D. 1077, p. 144.

other instances of endowments, made by the Hoysaḷa kings and their ministers for running charity houses in the 12th century. General Huḷḷa built an almshouse in 1163 at Jinanāthapura, a village about a mile from Śravaṇa-Beḷgola[1] In 1174 the Hoysaḷa king Ballāla II gave gifts of land and village Meruhaḷḷi for providing good food to the Jaina ascetics.[2] But the Nañjedevaraguḍḍa stone inscription of 1192[3] gives us most interesting details about the free distribution of food to the Jaina ascetics in the temple of the god Abhinava Śāntideva at Somepur in the Hassan district and furnishes clear proof of the interest taken both by the Hoysaḷa king and subjects in managing the affairs of charity house. As the king became pleased to see the good management of alms distribution, he also made a gift of two villages to Vajranandi-Siddhāntadeva for continuing this practice in the 12th century. It is clear from the above epigraphs that the Jaina charity houses took care of the Jaina ascetics as well as the poor and sick persons. They distributed food and water ; made provisions for feeding the visitors and provided shelter to them.

Pūjyapāda in his *Sarvārthasiddhi* defines *dāna* as the act of giving one's wealth to another for mutual benefit.[4] In his view, it accumulates religious merit for the donors and fosters the three jewels, right belief, right knowledge and right conduct, in others. Ravisena regards *dāna* as handing over of something of one's possession to the Jaina ascetics, and condemns other forms of charity as worthless and meaningless.[5] Somadeva too supports[6] the same view in his work.

Literary evidence regarding *dāna* is supplemented by the donative records of our period. They bear testimony to the fact that the devout Jainas made liberal donations of land, house and village at the request of their preceptors. The Noṇamaṅgala copper plate of the Gaṅga king Avinīta registers

1. *EC*, ii, SB 345, pp. 148-9.
2. Ibid. v, Cn. 146, pp. 188-9.
3. *MAR*, 1926, pp. 50-1.
4. *Sarvārthasiddhi*, ch. 7, v. 38, p. 372.
5. *Padmapurāṇa*, pt. i, ch. 14, v. 96, p. 313.
6. *Yaśastilaka*, pt. ii, BK. viii. p. 403.

the gift of the Veennelkarani village for the Uranūr Arhat temple and one fourth of the *kārṣāpaṇas* of the external customs for Perur Evāniaḍigale's Arhat temple on the advice of Vijayakīrti in the 5th century.[1] Another record of the same king records the gift of house at the village Pulliura for the Jaina monks of the Yāvanīka saṅgha in the 6th century.[2] In the 7th century, Vinayāditya gifted a village at the request of Dhurvadevācārya of the Mūlasaṅgha and Devagaṇa.[3] The Īcvāḍi stone inscription refers to the donation of money in cash and some wet-fields to Candra-Siddhāntadeva, a Jaina teacher of the Digambara sect in the 10th century.[4] In the 11th-12th centuries, many Jaina ladies of Karnataka gained prominence by making generous donation of the four gifts of food, medicine, shelter and learning. Caṭṭaladevī,[5] Lakṣmīmatī,[6] Pocikabbe,[7] Demiyakka[8] and Pampadevī[9] are depicted in the epigraphs as following the Jaina concept of *dāna*.

Although the traditional Jaina concept of the four gifts of protection, food, medicine, and sacred lore and writing materials continued to hold ground during the early medieval age, the gift of protection (*abhayadāna*) was considered to be the highest gift.[10] Apparently protection was emphasised in view of the political instability and frequent transfers of lands and villages from one hand to the other in early medieval times. A Jaina was therefore exhorted to offer protection to all living creatures without which the ritual of charity became meaningless. The next in importance was the gift of food. The Jainas were asked to feed the Jaina monks, according to the ninefold method of hospitality, consisting of reception, offering of a high seat, washing of their feet, adoration,

1. *EC*, x, ML. 72, p. 172.
2. *MAR*, 1938, p. 86.
3. *BKI*, iv, no. 4, p. 3.
4. *MAR*, 1923, p. 115.
5. *EC*, viii, Nr. 35, pp. 137-8.
6. Ibid. ii, SB. 127, p. 56.
7. Ibid. SB 118, pp. 48-9.
8. Ibid. SB 129, pp, 56-7.
9. Ibid. viii, Nr. 37, pp. 141-2
10. *Yaśastilaka*. pt. ii, BK. viii, p. 404.

salutation, purity of food, etc.[1] The gift of medicine and shelter was meant for the medical and physical care of the monks and saints.[2] Somadeva made it obligatory for the pious Jainas to help the monks in case of their physical and mental troubles. They were also advised to provide lodging, books and material for writing so that they might continue their spiritual concentration and fully explain the holy texts.[3]

We have already pointed out the growing importance of the gift of protection in the early Middle Ages. We also notice a few significant changes in the nature of other gifts during this period. Originally, the gift consisted mainly of pure food, a pot for answering the call of nature, peacock feather's broom, and materials necessary for the study of monks. But now the monks were being granted lands, houses and villages, which completely nullified their vow of non-possession. Ravisena in his *Padmapurāṇa* clearly states that the Jaina devotees should grant these objects on the ground of their connection with the Jinas. The gift of land and animal was supposed to confer permanent worldly pleasure on the donors.[4]

The Jaina texts speak of the three principal forms of charity, *sāttvika*, *tāmasa* and *rājasa*. Somadeva in his *yaśastilaka* explains each one of these. When a gift is made with devotion at a proper time to a worthy person by a donor equipped with seven qualities of faith, contentment, reverence, knowledge, liberality, forbearance and ability, it is called *sāttvika*.[5] The gift to an unworthy person who does not deserve any respect is called *tāmasa*.[6] The donation made for self-glorification without any faith is called *rājasa*.[7] Somadeva declares the *sāttvika* to be the best and condemns the other two. He adds that lack of

1. *Yaśastilaka*, pt. ii, BK. viii, p. 404.
2. Ibid. p. 409.
3. Ibid.
4. *Padmapurāṇa*, pt. i, ch. 14, vv. 78-80, p. 311.
5. *Yaśastilaka*, pt. ii, BK. viii, p. 408.
6. Ibid.
7. Ibid.

personal faith and punctuality, and jealousy at the generosity of others, etc., spoils charity.[1]

The Jainas are repeatedly warned against making gifts to undeserving persons. The Jaina texts from Karnataka declare the naked Jaina ascetics, who observe the vow of non-injury and practise austerities, to be the most deserving.[2] The gifts made to those who follow false doctrines and wrong conduct, produce evil consequences such as the feeding of serpents with milk[3] and are considered as futile as sowing seeds on stone. Somadeva shudders at the appearance of the Buddhists, Nāstikas, Śaivas and Ājīvikas at the reception of the Jaina monks because it leads to pollution.[4] In the *Ādipurāṇa*, the prince Bharata is said to have refused charity to those who violated the vow of non-injury.[5] Somadeva classifies the worthy recipients into five categories.[6] They are *samayin* or adherent of the Jaina faith, the *śrāvaka* or, one who has an expert knowledge of astrology, incantations and omens, the *sādhu* who has mastered religious austerities and observed all the Jaina religious vows, the *sūri* or the instructor, and the *samayadipaka* or one who advances the cause of the Jaina faith.

Begging and Dietary Practices of the Jaina Monks

The sacred injunction that forbade the Jaina monks to cook their food themselves made it compulsory for them to go on regular tour for begging food except in the four months of the rainy season.

Purity of food and abstaining from night's meal both for the monks and the laymen continued to be stressed in the Jaina circles during the early medieval age. In order to maintain the Jaina vow of non-injury, Ravisena in his

1. *Yaśastilaka*, pt, ii, BK. viii, p. 410.
2. *Padmapurāṇa*, pt. i, ch. 14, vv. 53-8, pp. 309-10;
   Ādipurāṇa, pt.i, ch. 20. vv. 146-8, pp. 458;
   Varāṅgacarita, ch. 7, v. 31, p. 62.
3. *Yaśastilaka*, cited in K.K. Handiqui, op. cit, p. 284.
4. Ibid.
5. *Ādipurāṇa*, pt. ii, ch. 38, vv. 10-18. pp. 240-1.
6. K.K. Handiqui, op. cit., pp. 284-5.

Padmapurāṇa denounced the practice of taking meal at night.[1] Like the *Mūlācāra*, the *Padmapurāṇa* and other Jaina texts enjoin the monks to take food in their palms in a standing position.[2] The *Varāṅgacarita* states that the Jaina monks do not accept food brought to them or especially prepared for them ; nor do they take relishing food such as *ghī*, milk, salt, sugar and oil.[3] The monks eat not for acquiring strength, increasing longevity and gratifying their taste but for sustaining life so that they might carry on constant study and practise austerities. Guṇabhadra in his *Ātmānuśāsana* praises those monks who abide by the rules laid down in the Jaina *āgamas*. Such monks accept food with devotion from the Jaina householders to keep their body and soul together.[4]

Similarly the medieval texts repeat and reflect on the old rules regarding begging. The *Varāṅgacarita*[5] informs us that some monks pledged to accept food from only six or seven householders. If they failed to procure food, they went back without food. They did not stay in a village for more than one day and five days in a town. Sometimes they reduced the prescribed quantity of food to less than half and kept themselves hungry.[6] The *Yaśastilaka* refers to roving groups of monks under the sage Sudatta and describes them as observing the Jaina vows, known as the *samitis* and *guptis*.[7]

These details prove beyond doubt the rigid observances of dietary practices by the Jaina monks. But we also notice certain new practices. In some cases, the Jaina monks adopted flexibility and slackness in dietary practices. Though the wandering monks continued to be puritan, the monks who settled

1. *Padmapurāṇa*, pt. i, ch. 14. vv. 268ff, pp. 325-6.
2. Cf. *Mūlācāra*, pt. ii, v. 54, p. 59.
3. *Varāṅgacarita*, ch. 30, vv. 57-8, p. 298; *Padmapurāṇa*, pt. i, ch. 4, vv. 95-7, p.64.
4. *Ātmānuśāsana*, v. 158, p. 149.
5. *Varāṅgacarita*, ch. 30, vv. 54-5, p. 298.
6. The *Mūlācāra* states that the monk should fill half of his stomach with food, one fourth with water and one fourth with air. The quantity of food was thirtytwo morsels, Cf. *Mūlācāra*, 6.72. ibid. 5, 153, cited in S.B. Deo, op. cit., p. 344.
7. *Yaśastilaka*, BK i, pp. 50-1.

permanently in the Jaina monasteries and managed the affairs of the Jaina temples became lax. Somadeva states that while giving food it is useless to examine whether the monks are good or bad; the householder is purified by the mere act of making the gift.[1] He also encourages the wealthy Jainas to extend charities to the Jaina monk whether he conforms to the standard laid down in the Jaina scriptures or not.[2]

Evidently some Jaina monks had deviated from the original standard. On the ground of their conduct and character they did not deserve food and other gifts. Somadeva tried to save the situation by diverting attention from the worthiness of the monks to the virtues of making gifts. Guṇabhadra too complains against the loose dietary practices. He ridicules the corrupt monks who admire those householders who offer good dishes and condemn those who offer poor food. He underlines the absence of good monks and attributes it to the effect of bad times.[3] The *Padmapurāṇa* states at several places that the Jaina monks accept tasty food[4] and that they do not observe the vow of silence during the time of taking meal. Contrary to the old rules, they grant boon to the devotee and make predictions in order to please their clients.[5]

The slackness which crept into the dietary practices of the Jaina monks of Karnataka was the result of settled monastic life. Permanent residence in the monasteries encouraged them to follow corrupt practices without caring for the old rules.

The practice of rain retreat

The traditional custom of observing *caturmāsa* or staying at one place for four months in the rainy season continued to prevail among the Jainas of Karnataka, as is indicated by the Jaina epigraphs and literary texts. An epigraph of the 6th

1. *Yaśastilaka*, pt. ii, BK. viii, p. 407, cited in K.K. Handiqui, op. cit., p 285.
2. Ibid.
3. *Ātmānuśāsana*, v. 159, pp. 150-1.
4. *Padmapurāṇa*, pt. ii, ch. 41, vv. 25-6, p. 200; ibid. pt. iii, ch. 85, vv. 143ff. p. 146.
5. Ibid. pt. ii, 41, v. 112, p. 206.

century informs us that the Kadamba king Ravivarmā granted land for the support of the ascetics during the four months of the rainy season.[1] Another record of the 9th century refers to the observance of this practice by Bālakartar bhaṭāra.[2] Similarly the Jaina *Purāṇas* are replete with references to the rain retreat by the Jaina monks.

Although the practice of rain retreat is not peculiar to the Jainas alone,[3] they attach great importance to its observance because of their emphasis on the Jaina vow of non-injury, which made it compulsory for them to restrict their movements in order to avoid injury to the innumerable small insects that spring into life in the rainy season. The practice is also deemed beneficial to the lay community. During their stay, the monks redress the grievances of the laymen who render all facilities to them.[4]

The monks pay particular attention to the selection of the place of residence during the rainy season. Generally, they prefer to stay in a lonely place, free from living creatures. Ravisena states that the monks live during the rains in the caves or on the bank of the river or in the Jaina temples.[5] He further tells us that it commences with the fullmoon day of Āṣāḍha (June-July) and ends with the fullmoon day of Kārttika (October-November).[6] Continuous fasting and meditation appear to be the chief concern of the Jaina monks during the period of their stay.

Jaina Penance

The significant position of penance in the life of a Jaina monk is duly emphasised in the literary and epigraphic sources of early medieval Karnataka. Regular penance is held essential

1. *IA*, vi, no. 22. p. 27.
2. *BKI*, i, pt. i, no. 18, p. 11.
3. The rule regarding the suspension of wanderings during the rainy season occurs among the regulations of different sects; the Buddhists call it *vāsa* and the Brāhmaṇical Sannyāsins are enjoined to remain in fixed residence (*Dhurvaśilā*) during the time. Cited in S. K. Dutt, *Buddhist monks and monasteries of India*, p. 53.
4. S. B. Deo, op. cit., p. 340.
5. *Padmapurāṇa*, pt. iii, ch. 92, vv. 17-8, p. 177.
6. Ibid, pt.i, ch. 22, v. 66, p. 463 and v. 83, p. 464.

for the purification of the soul, perverted through human actions and evil activities, such as cruelty, greediness and deceitfulness. The accumulation of evil actions retards the progress of the soul towards spiritual liberation. The penance annihilates worldly desires and destroys attachment to the things of this transitory universe.

The twofold division of Jaina penance into external (*bāhya*) and internal (*abhyantara*), and the proliferation of each into six forms remained unchanged during the early medieval age. The *Sarvārthasiddhi* of Pūjyapāda, assigned to the 5th-6th centuries, enumerates all these twelve forms of Jaina austerities and their subdivisions.[1]

The external penance includes fasting (*anaśana*), eating less than one desires (*avamaudarya*), taking a mental vow to accept food only if certain conditions are fulfilled *vṛttiparisaṅkhyāna*), the abandonment of delicious food such as *ghī*, sugar, salt, milk, butter and oil (rasaparityāga), sleeping and sitting in a lonely place devoid of living beings (*viviktaśayyāsana*), and the mortification of the body (*Kāyakleśa*). These six forms are intended to purify the sense organs on the one hand and lessen the sense of attachment to the objects of worldly enjoyments on the other. They are chiefly concerned with the control of bodily activities. Their performance is also necessary for the attainment of perfection in the practices of internal penance.

The internal penance consists of expiations (*prāyaścittas*), reverence for the three jewels of right conduct, right belief and right knowledge (*vinaya*), serving and attending upon the old, infirm and holy saints (*vaiyāvṛtya*), non-attachment to the body (*vyutsarga*), study of the Jaina scriptures (*svādhyāya*), and meditation (*dhyāna*). All these are concerned with the control of the mental activities.[2]

The Jaina epigraphs support the literary texts in respect of the various forms of Jaina penance. A Śravaṇa-Beḷgoḷa record of the 8th century informs us of the observance of the

1. *Sarvārthasiddhi*, ch. 9, vv. 19-20, pp. 438-9;
   Dravya Saṅgraha, v. 35., p. 87;
   Varāṅgacarita, ch. 31, vv. 71-3, p. 307.
2. *Sarvārthasiddhi*, ch. 9, v. 20, p. 439.

twelve kinds of penance by the nun Anantamatī-ganti in consonance with the prescribed rules.[1] Similar other inscriptions at Śravaṇa-Beḷgoḷa refer to the value of penance,[2] meditation[3] and fasting. Besides mentioning the traditional twelve kinds of Jaina austerities, an epigraph of the 8th century refers to a monk who practised severe penance for one hundred and eight years; this was as difficult as walking on the sharp edge of a sword or on fire or passing over the great fangs of a cobra.[4]

Of the six kinds of external penance, fasting appears to be the most important not only for the Jaina monks but also for the householders. The teachers of Digambara school evolved an elaborate system of fasting and prescribed various rules for its proper observance by the Jainas of Karnataka in early medieval times. Pūjyapāda states that fast secures self-control, exterminates attachment, and acquires spiritual knowledge.[5]

Jinasena Sūri in his *Harivaṁśapurāṇa* gives us a detailed and exhaustive list of fasts to be undertaken regularly. He enumerates as many as forty types of fasts, differing in regard to method and duration. He refers first to the *sarvatobhadra-upavāsa*,[6] which lasts one hundred days. The Jainas are asked to observe fast for one day in the beginning and then gradually increase its duration from one to two, three, four and five days. The next type of fasting is called the *vasantabhadra upavāsa*, lasting for thirtyfive days. In course of this fast one is allowed to take a meal on the sixth, thirteenth, twenty first, thirtieth and fortieth day.[7] In the *Ekāvali* form of fasting, one fasts for twenty four days; each fast is followed by a meal day.[8] According to Jinasena Sūri, one attains the merits of god Jinendra or becomes a Jaina prophet, if a Jaina practises *Jinendraguṇasampatti* fast, which continues for a hundred and twenty six days, every

1. *EC.* ii. SB. 23, p.6.; ibid, SB. 98, p.43.
2. Ibid. SB 75, p. 40; ibid. SB. 76, 41.
3. Ibid. SB. 81, p. 41.
4. *EC*, ii, SB. 22, pp. 5-6.
5. *Sarvārthasiddhi*, ch. 3, v. 19, p. 438.
6. *Harivaṁśapurāṇa*, pt. ii, ch. 34, vv. 52-5, pp. 434-5.
7. Ibid. v. 56, p. 435.
8. Ibid. v. 67, p. 436.

fasting day alternating with a meal day.[1] Finally, the Jaina texts refer to fasts, lasting for the period of five, six or twelve years. In the *Dharmacakra* type of fasting, one continues to fast for one thousand days. Since every fasting day alternates with a meal day, the process of fasting has to be completed in two thousand days.[2]

Monks, nuns, laymen and laywomen practise severe fasts of various magnitudes till their death for obtaining spiritual liberation. The practice of fast becomes so important in Karnataka that some of the Jaina monks style themselves as *upavāsapara*[3] (devoted to fasts) and *aṣṭopavāsa*[4] (one who fasts for eight days). The former is recorded as the disciple of Vṛṣabhanandi, and the latter is said to have erected memorial tomb for his teacher *Elācārya*.

Most fasts are possibly prescribed for the Jaina ascetics who aspire to combat the grosser desires of the body so as to prepare it for some sacred ideals. Ordinary fasts form a part of the preparation for the final fast unto death. The provision for taking meals at intervals appears to be a common feature of all the above forms, and is essential for their sustenance so that they may continue their ascetic practices. But they clearly show that the Jaina monks lead a rigorous life of self-abnegation and try to control their sense organs by practising the austerity of fasting. Though the Jaina texts prescribe fasts that extend for a period of five or six or twelve years, epigraphic sources mention only such fasts as lasted for five days, twelve days, twenty one days, one month and two months. It seems possible that fasts of longer duration had gone out of vogue or they were presented as ideals which could never be realised. The post-canonical literature of the *Śvetāmbaras* does also lament the disappearance of longer fasts among the Śvetāmbaras.[5]

The Jaina laity, men and women, are also enjoined to

1. *Harivaṁśapurāṇa*, pt. ii, ch. 34, v. 122, p, 445.
2. Ibid. p. 443, cited by Pannalal Jain, (ed.), *Harivaṁśapurāṇa*.
3. *EC,* ii, SB. 75, p. 40.
4. *MAR.* 1914, p. 38.
5. Cf. Deo S. B., op. cit., p. 419.

observe fasting. The main objects are almost the same as in the case of ascetics. But householders, unlike the Jaina monks, practise them also for the attainment of temporal benefits such as good health and religious merit. Fasts on the seventh day of the bright fortnight of the month of Bhādra (August-September) every year and the eleventh day of the dark fortnight of every month are calculated to bring endless happiness to the pious devotees.[1] Jinasena in his *Ādipurāṇa* emphasises the need of performing fasts for acquiring good health and curing diseases caused by respiration and gall-bladder.[2] Besides fasting on some auspicious days, the Jaina householders are also advised to abstain from food for four days every month. Fasting on the eighth and the fourteenth lunar days in each fortnight, known as the *proṣodhaupavāsa* in the Jaina literature, is especially recommended for the laity.[3] The process of the fast involves the giving up of bath and bodily decoration including garlands, perfumes and ornaments.[4] This fast has to be carried on at some sacred place such as the abode of a saint or on a hill or at home or in the Jaina temples, where the devotees are asked to engage in religious meditation[5] all the time; they have to concentrate on pure thought. The purification of the inner spirit[6] is thought to be a compulsory ingredient of this fast and it cannot be obtained without the mortification of the body. It is apparent that laymen are supposed to lead the life of a monk at least for a limited period by giving up all sinful actions and family life, which retard the progress of the soul towards perfection.

Three other kinds of external penance are also concerned with the diet control. They appear to be supplementary vows to serve the needs of fasting. The *Kāyakleśa* or mortification of the body is prescribed for enduring physical pain and abandoning worldly comforts. The *Varāṅgacarita* refers to prince

1. *Harivaṁśapurāṇa*, pt. ii, ch. 34, vv. 126-8, pp. 445-6.
2. *Ādipurāṇa*, pt. i, ch. 20, v. 7, p. 445.
3. *Varāṅgacarita*, ch. 15, v. 123, p. 139; *Sarvārthasiddhi*, pt. ii, ch. 58, v. 154, p. 679.
4. *Yaśastilaka*, pt. ii, BK. viii, p. 402.
5. Ibid.
6. Ibid.

Varāṅga who performs various bodily austerities without caring for heat, cold and continuous raining.[1] He practises austerities under a tree in desolate, forbidding place, on the burial ground, and also in a standing position facing the sun for the whole day.[2] The mortification of the body is held as important a penance as the head among the different organs of the body.[3]

The six kinds of internal penance are concerned with the control of mental activities.[4] Of them the last called *dhyāna* or meditation is the most important. It is considered to be the best means of securing emancipation from worldly bondage. It helps the practitioner to understand the true nature of the soul and to distinguish it from the human body. According to the Jaina doctrines, the soul has inherent capacity for liberation, but it is obstructed by the evil actions. Thus the Jaina teachers Pūjyapāda, Yogīndudeva, Śubhacandra and Somadeva thoroughly explain the method of self-realization in their respective works such as *Samādhiśataka*, *Paramātmaprakāśa*, *Jñānārṇava* and the *Yaśastilaka*. They suggest various means for contemplation by diverting attention from the external objects of the world.

Pūjyapāda defines *dhyāna* as the concentration of mind on a particular object by a person of excellent physique. As equanimity cannot be quickly attained, the longest duration of meditation is stated to be an *antaramuhūrta*, that is for a period of forty-eight minutes.[5]

The primary objects of meditation are explained in the early Digambara texts. The twelve topics for meditation, known as the *anuprekṣas* or reflections on the twelve items in Jaina philosophy, figure prominently without any alterations in the Jaina literature of Karnataka during early medieval times. Both Somadeva and Śubhacandra throw sufficient light

1. *Varāṅgacarita*, ch. 30, vv. 26ff, pp. 295ff.
2. Ibid.
3. *Ādipurāṇa*, pt. i, ch. 20, vv. 181-3, p. 462.
4. *Sarvārthasiddhi*, ch. 9, v. 20, p. 439.
5. *Sarvārthasiddhi*, ch. 9, v. 27, p. 444.
   Jñānārṇava, ch. 2, vv. 8ff, pp. 17ff.
   Dravya saṅgraha, v. 35, p. 88.

on the twelve objects of meditation in the beginning stage. They include reflection on the fleeting nature of things, the sense of helplessness, the cycle of worldly transmigration, the loneliness of worldly sojourn, the distinctness of the soul from the body, the impure condition of the body, the nature of the universe, etc.[1]

The supreme object of meditation, according to Jaina philosophers, is the contemplation of the transcendental soul which is free from all blemishes and impurities.[2] It is not the universal soul of the Vedānta but the pure and all-knowing soul in each individual, circumscribed and obscured for the time being by the hindrances of human actions.[3] It is essential to note here that Jaina philosophers clearly speak of three states of the soul, the outer soul (*bahirātmā*), inner soul (*antarātmā*) and the transcendental soul (paramātmā).[4] They agree with the famous teacher Kundakunda that the outer soul consists of the sense organs ; the internal soul is the consciousness which distinguishes itself from the body ; and the transcendental soul is the emancipated soul free from all impurities.[5]

Dhyāna is broadly classified into two main categories ; *apraśastadhyāna* (inauspicious) and *praśastadhyāna* (auspicious).[6] Whereas the former is the cause of mundane sufferings, the latter, the sole penance for removing them, leads to spiritual liberation. These two categories are further subdivided into four forms, namely the mournful (*ārta*), cruel (*raudra*), virtuous (*dharma*) and the pure meditation (*śukladhyāna*).[7] The former two types of Jaina meditation should be avoided because they create sufferings and raise obstacles in the path of liberation,

1. *Yaśastilaka*, pt. i, BK. ii, vv. 105ff, pp. 256ff;
   Jñānārṇava, ch. 2, vv. 8ff, pp. 17ff;
   Dravya Saṅgraha, v. 35, p. 88.
2. *Jñānārṇava*, ch. 32, v. 32, p. 314; *Yogasāra*, v. 5, p. 372.
3. K. K. Handiqui, op. cit ,p. 273.
4. *Paramātmaprakāśa*, p. 20; *Samādhitantra*, v. 4, p. 8.
5. K. K. Handiqui, op. cit., p. 273.
6. *Jñānārṇava*, ch. 25. v. 17, p. 256; *Ādipurāṇa*, pt. i, ch. 21, v. 27, p. 477.
7. *Sarvārthasiddhi*, ch. 9, v. 28, p. 445; *Yaśastilaka*, pt. ii, p. 393; *Jñānārṇava*, ch. 25, v. 20, p. 256.

but the last two forms are considered capable of securing the final liberation.[1]

Constant thinking over unpleasant objects such as enmity, poison, weapons, etc. and the anxiety to get rid of them; the separation of the desired objects such as son, wife and wealth and the intense longing for them; the anxiety to remove pain and disease; and the feelings for the enjoyment of unsatisfied desires are the four characteristics of the mournful meditation.[2] The *raudra* or cruel meditation implies the absorption of mind in *hiṁsā* (injury) and other forms of sin such as falsehood, theft, and the protection of the means of enjoyment.[3] Taking into consideration the nature of the above two kinds of meditation, the Jaina thinkers condemn them as essentially evil. Indeed, the performance of these two forms is bound to bring inauspicious results for the meditators. They convey a general impression of worldly attachment, which is detrimental to the progress of soul towards liberation.

The four objects of virtuous meditation[4] are the pure and infallible revelation of truth based on absolute faith in the Jaina scriptures (*ājñāvicaya*); the fact of the universal sufferings and its conditions (*apāyavicaya*); the nature and consequence of the fruition of various actions (*vipākavicaya*) and the structure of the universe. Śubhacandra states that friendship with all creatures, appreciation of the merits of others, sympathy and compassion for others, and the indifference to unruly are the necessary conditions for attaining success in the practice of virtuous meditation.[5]

The *śukladhyāna* or pure meditation signifies unbroken contemplation of one's own *ātmā* or soul. It is recognized as the highest form of Jaina contemplation. Somadeva in his *Yaśastilaka* points out the four stages in this meditation. These are also corroborated by the *Jñānārṇava* which deals with the Jaina Yoga. In the first stage, the meditator concentrates his mind on the different aspects of the universal objects from

1. *Jñānārṇava*, ch. 25, V. 20, p. 256.
2. Ibid., ch. 25, vv. 24ff, pp. 257ff; *Sarvārthasiddhi*, ch. 9, vv. 30-3, pp. 446-7.
3. Ibid. ch. 9, v. 35, p. 448.
4. Ibid. v. 36, p. 449.
5. *Jñānārṇava*, ch. 27, v. 4, p. 272.

various standpoints. As the mind does not concentrate on a particular object, it is known as the *pṛthaktvavitarkavicāra*. In the second stage, he turns his mind to a single object without any change; hence it is known as the *ekatvavitarkavicāra*. In the *sūkṣmakriyā-pratipāti* (contemplation accompanied with subtle physical movements) all the mental activities and the working of the sense organs are stopped except some minute vibration in the soul itself. In the fourth stage, even the remaining subtle activities of the soul come to a stop, and the soul becomes completely motionless.[1] This makes the consummation of pure meditation, and the devotee attains final liberation from the worldly transmigration.

According to Somadeva, five factors contribute towards Yoga. They are indifference to the world, maturity of knowledge, lack of attachment, a steadfast mind and ability to endure the privations of hunger, thirst, grief, old age and death. The obstacles to Yoga, according to him, are mental suffering, disease, error, carelessness, idleness, attachment and fickleness. One who practises Yoga should be free from anger and pleasure and remain impervious, like a clod of earth, both to one who pierces him with thorns and one who smears him with the sandal paste.[2]

The role of bodily postures (*āsana*) for securing perfect steadiness in contemplation even in the face of adventitious obstacles[3] is duly emphasised by the Jaina teachers of Karnataka. Various postures such as *Vīrāsana* or the hero-posture, *padmāsana* or sitting with crossed legs, etc., are prescribed to lessen constant fatigue and the mental diversions, which impair meditation. Śubhacandra strongly recommends the adoption of *padmāsana* and the *kāyotsarga* for the meditators of the present age.[4] He adds that the monks of earlier times obtained salvation by practising *vajrāsana* and *kamalāsana* which were far more difficult.[5] He draws a beautiful picture

1. *Jñānārṇava* ch. 41, vv. 7ff , pp. 431 ff.
2. *Yaśastilaka*, pt ii, BK. viii, p. 393, cited in K.K. Handiqui, op. cit., p. 275.
3. *Jñānārṇava*, ch. 28, vv. 30ff, pp. 282ff.
4. Ibid. v. 12, p. 279.
5. Ibid., v. 10, p. 278.

of a meditator, engrossed in self-concentration. He dives deep into the ocean of love and sympathy for all creatures, and is absolutely free from attachment to the world. He keeps his body straight and erect, and becomes as motionless as a painted figure.[1] The withdrawal of the mind along with the sense organs from the external objects (*pratyāhāra*) and its concentration (*dhāraṇā*) on some place of the body, for instance, the forehead, is essential to the development of the power of contemplation.[2]

We may notice several points of resemblance between the Yoga system of Patañjali and the Jaina Yoga. Patañjali's Yoga stands for the restraint of the sense organs and the mind.[3] Emphasis on the observance of the moral and physical discipline, bodily postures, breath-control and withdrawal of the senses from their natural and outward functions are indispensable for spiritual progress. They are decidedly a common feature of both the systems. The moral virtues of the Jainas can be compared with the five types of *niyama* (observance) recommended by Patañjali.

1. Ibid. ch. 28, vv. 34ff, pp, 283ff.
2. Ibid. ch. 30, v. 13, p. 307.
3. S. Radhakrishnan, *Indian Philosophy*, ii, p. 338.

CHAPTER V

ORIGIN AND GROWTH OF JAINA MONACHISM IN KARNATAKA

Jaina monachism means the collective life of the monks and nuns organised at a fixed place where they live together under one authority for spiritual liberation. It appears to be the most important development in Karnataka during early medieval times.

The earlier Jaina monks led a wandering life throughout the year except the four months of the rainy season when they lived at a fixed abode. The early texts of both the Śvetāmbaras and the Digambaras frankly recommend solitary life for the Jaina ascetics, who aspired to attain salvation. The *Mūlācāra* and the *Pravacanasāra*, which were composed roughly in the beginning of the Christian era,[1] oppose the permanent habitation of monks at one place for a long time. The former states that the monk should stay in a deserted house or under a tree or on burial grounds or in caves.[2] They are further ordained to avoid such places as were especially built for them and were likely to arouse their passions[3] and present obstacles in the path of spiritual liberation.

The transition from solitary wandering to settled life in Jaina monasteries and Jaina *basadis* was a striking development in the history of Jainism in Karnataka. The Jaina epigraphs, which record donation for the erection of monasteries and temples, show that the practice of permanent settlement of the Jaina monks in monasteries had begun in the last quarter of the 4th century. In 370 the Gaṅga king Mādhava converted the Kumarāpura village into a freehold for the use of the monks who probably lived in the monastery attached to

1. Cf. A.N. Upadhye, (ed.), *Pravacanasāra*, Introd. p. xxii.
2. *Mūlācāra*, 9. 21, 22, cited in S.B. Deo, op. cit., p. 342.
3. Ibid. 10.58, p, 342.

the Jina temple which was established by the Mūla saṅgha; the gift was made at the instance of ācārya Vīradeva.[1]

From the 5th century onwards, numerous epigraphs show that the Jaina monasteries were being built by the side of the Jaina temples in the different parts of Mysore by the pious Jaina devotees. They displayed great enthusiasm in donating large tracts of land and villages for the proper maintenance of those monasteries and the monks and nuns living therein.

The relation between the Jaina monasteries and the Jaina temples should be made clear at the very outset. The Jaina monasteries in Karnataka were generally a composite structure, incorporating the Jaina *maṭhas* and the Jaina temples within its fold. They could not be distinguished from the Jaina temples in Karnataka. We have only a few separate Jaina *maṭhas* serving exclusively as residences of monks and nuns; generally they were attached to the Jaina temples. The Jaina monasteries in Karnataka did not possess the grandeur of such Buddhist vihāras as that of Nalanda which contained temples, colleges and the congregational buildings beside the residence of the Buddhist bhikṣus.

From the 5th century, Jaina monasteries in Karnataka began to multiply. An epigraph, dated 425, records the donation of the village Vennelkarani in the Korikunda viśaya for the benefit of the monks living in the monastery attached to the Uranur Arhat temple, established by Candranandī and others of the Śrī-Mūla saṅgha. This was done on the advice of the preceptor Vijayakīrti.[2] In 466 the Gaṅga king Avinīta presented the charming village named Badaneguppe in the Chamarajnagar taluq of Mysore to the Śrīvijaya Jaina temple of Talavananagara or the modern Talakad, situated on the bank of the Kaveri in the south-west of the Mysore district.[3] The same Gaṅga king made several endowments in the 6th century. In 570 he gave wet fields and a house situated near the Jaina temple at the village Pullura where the monks of

1. *EC*, ML 73, pp. 171-3.
2. Ibid, x, ML 72, p. 172.
3. Ibid, i, Cg. 1, p. 51.

the Yāvanika saṅgha lived.[1]

Regular subsidies for the maintenance of different sects of the Digambaras were provided by the Kadamba kings of western Mysore. Mṛgeśavarmā built a Jaina temple at Palāśika or modern Halsi in the Belgaum district and granted several *nivartanas* of land for the benefit of the Yāpanīya, the Nirgrantha and the Kūrcaka sects who probably resided in the same temple.[2] The endowment was increased by Harivarmā who gave the village Vasantavāṭaka to the Kūrcakas for meeting their annual expenses at the eight day festival of the Jaina temple which Mṛgeśavarmā had built at Palāśika. The balance of the grant was to be spent on feeding the whole sect of the Digambaras in the 6th century.[3] Harivarmā also granted the village of Marade for the use of the holy people who lived in the Jaina temple at Palāśika.[4]

The Jaina teachers of Karnataka exploited the simple faith of the Jaina laity and encouraged them to erect more *maṭhas* which were declared to be essential for the attainment of temporal as well as the eternal bliss. This is evident from the study of the *Padmapurāṇa*, the *Varāṅgacarita*, the *Ādipurāṇa*, etc., which were composed in Karnataka in between the 8th and 9th centuries.

The Jaina monasteries multiplied fast in subsequent centuries. No less than sixty-five monastic establishments are recorded during the 7th-10th centuries. In 634 the Jaina poet Ravikīrti constructed a Jaina temple at Aihoḷe in the Bijapur district, and it was granted land by Pulakeśin II.[5] In 776 as many as thirty one house sites along with a house were granted for the construction of new quarters of the monks and nuns attached to the Lokatilaka Jinālaya, located in the city of Śrīpura. It was also given land with varying irrigational facilities such as six *kaṇḍugas* of black soil under the big tank and two *kaṇḍugas* of rice land in the Sripura plain.[6] In 859

1. *MAR*, 1938, p. 86.
2. *IA*, vi, no. 21, p. 25.
3. Ibid. no. 25, p. 31.
4. Ibid, vi, no. 26, pp. 31-2.
5. *EI*, vi, p. 12.
6. *EC*, iv, Ng. 85, pp. 134-5.

the Nāgula Jaina monastery was built by Nagallura Pollabbe and endowed with two *mattars* of land and a house site; Naganandyācārya of the Singhāvura gaṇa received the gift.[1] The Śāntara king Tolapuruṣa Vikrama Śāntara built a stone *basadi* for Moni-Siddhānta-bhaṭāra of the Kondakundānvaya.[2] It was evidently used as a dwelling place in the 9th century. The Gaṅga king Śivamāra II built the Śivamāra *basadi* at Śravaṇa-Beḷgoḷa in 810.[3] About the same time, the younger brother of Śivamāra II also gave specified land to the *koil-basadi*. The same *basadi* received land from the inhabitants of three villages.[4]

The 10th century was remarkable for the erection of several new monasteries in Karnataka. An undated stone inscription, assigned to the 10th century, mentions the gift of wet fields by the Gaṅga King Nanniya Gaṅga and his queen to Candrasiddhāntadeva, a Jaina teacher of the Digambara sect. His wife offered money for the worship of the Jina in the Jaina temple.[5] The famous Jaina teacher Muñjārya Vādighangala Bhaṭṭa received an endowment of the village Bagiyūr from the Gaṅga king Mārasiṁha II. The income from the village amounted to 20 *gadyāṇas* in cash and 12 *kaṇḍugas* in grain.[6] In A.D. 980 the Raṭṭa chief Śāntivarma gave 150 *mattars* of land to the Jaina *basadi* built by him at Saundatti; the gift was entrusted to Bāhubali-bhaṭṭāraka.[7] His mother Nijiyabbarasi also granted 150 *mattars* of land to the same Jaina sanctuary. Bhimarasibhaṭāra received land and money for imparting instruction (*vidyā-dāna*) and for meeting the expenses of the *maṭha* attached to the Jaina temple at Soratur in the district of Dharwar.[8] Regular supply of food to the Jaina *maṭha* at Sujingallu in the Bellary district was provided by a certain Cangagāvuṇḍa during the reign of the Rāṣṭrakūṭa

1. *KI*, ii, no. 5, p. 16.
2. *EC*, viii, Nr. 60, p. 154.
3. Ibid. ii, SB 415, p. 81.
4. *MAR*, 1932, pp, 240-1.
5. Ibid. 1923, p. 115.
6. Ibid. 1921, pp. 23-4.
7. *JBBRAS*, x, pp. 204ff.
8. *BKI*, i, pt. i, no. 39, p. 24.

king Kṛṣṇa III through an endowment made to Satyārasibhaṭāra.[1] In 968 the wife of the feudatory chief Paṇḍiga erected a monastery at Kākambal and granted it two villages, Madalūr and Malagavāḍi, converting them into freehold estates.[2]

Monarchs as well as the people of Karnataka continued the tradition of erecting monasteries and endowing them with rich gifts of land and village for their maintenance in the 11th-12th centuries. Two stone inscriptions from Kogali in the Bellary district demonstrate the Jaina leanings of the later Cālukya king Someśvara I. The first record, which is undated, registers the gift of land for the Cenna Pārśva *basadi*. In another record of 1055-6 the same king is recorded to have donated land for the Jaina ascetic Indrakīrti.[3] The Bandaṇike *basti* inscription of 1075[4] refers to Someśvara II's endowment of land for the Śāntinātha *basadi* in the Shikarpur taluq. Kulacandradeva of the Mūla saṅgha and Krāṇūrgaṇa is recorded to have received the gift. The Hoysaḷa kings also figure in the epigraphs as the builders of Jaina monasteries. In the Gandhavāraṇa *basti* inscription, dated 1131,[5] Vinayāditya II is recorded to have made a number of Jaina *basadis* at Śravaṇa-Beḷgoḷa. In 1133[6] and 1136,[7] Viṣṇuvardhana Deva is said to have donated the village of Jāvagal for the Vijaya Pārśvadeva Jinālaya and built a Jaina temple known as Viṣṇuvardhana-Jinālaya in Dorasamudra.

The common people, on the other hand, are also noted for similar attempts of temple construction. Govadeva, a feudatory chief, builds a Jaina temple at Heggere in the Tumkur district, for which his son donates land for eight kinds of worship and for providing food to the ascetics in 1160.[8] In the same year the Hoysaḷa gāvuṇḍa also builds a Jaina *basadi*

1. *Top. List of Inscriptions*, i, p. 265.
2. *EC*, xi, Cd. 14, p. 16.
3. B.A. Saletore, op. cit., p. 53.
4. *EC*, vii, Sk. 221, p. 131.
5. Ibid. ii, SB. 143, pp. 70-1.
6. Ibid. v, BL 124, p. 83.
7. Ibid. BL 17, pp. 48-51.
8. Ibid. xii, Ck, 21; pp. 77-8.

and endows it with grant of land.[1] Another record of 1173[2] registers the grant of a gift for the *basadi* in Kolgana by the farmers of Idaināḍ in the Chamrajnagar taluq of the Mysore district.

In course of time some Jaina monasteries came to assume authority over other religious establishments. An inscription speaks of such a monastery at Śravaṇa-Beḷgoḷa in the Hassan district of Mysore. This *maṭha* was founded in 982[3] by Cāmuṇḍarāya, the military general of the Gaṅga king Mārasiṁha II, who is said to have erected in the following year the famous colossal statue of Gommaṭeśvara on the Vindhyagiri hill.[4] It became the chief centre of the Jaina pontificates, which claimed authority over the Jainas throughout south India.[5] It was the place from where the Jainas extended their religious activities in the different parts of Karnataka. The shrine continues to be important even now not only for the Jainas of the south but also of Northern India. The Maleyur *maṭha*, which is now closed, was subordinate to that of Śravaṇa-Belgola. Akalaṅka, the famous logician who confuted the Buddhists at the court of Hemasitala in Kāñci in 788 and procured their expulsion from the south, is known to have hailed from Śravaṇa-Beḷgoḷa, but a manuscript which was in possession of Rice, states that he was monk of Maleyūr and that Bhaṭṭākalaṅka was the title of the line of teachers who lived in the *maṭha* of Maleyūr in the district of Mysore.[6] The foundation of the Humcca *maṭha*, which is still in existence in the Nagar taluq of the Shimoga district, was laid by Jinadatta Rāya during the 8th-9th centuries, who carved out the kingdom of the Śāntaras in the south. It became the chief centre of the goddess Padmāvatī who figures in the records of the 10th-11th centuries.[7]

1. *EC*, iv, Md. 69, pp. 12-3.
2. Ibid. iv, Ch. 181, p. 22.
3. Ibid. ii, SB 122, p. 50.
4. Ibid. SB 175, p. 89.
5. *Mysore Gazetteer*, i, p. 287.
6. Ibid. i, p. 288.
7. *EC*, x, Gd 4, p. 211; ibid. x, Sp. 64, p. 281.

Mulgund in the Gadug taluq of the Dharwar district also developed as a renowned centre of the Sena lineage, which wielded considerable influence upon the Jainas in Karnataka during the 9th-11th centuries. Ajitasena, Kanakasena and Nagasena, all of whom contributed to the diffusion of the Jaina culture in Karnataka, are known to have hailed from this place. An inscription of 902-3 speaks of Cīkārya, son of Candrārya of the vaiśya caste, who built a Jaina sanctuary at Mulgund. His son made an endowment of land for the upkeep of the establishment. Another piece of land was bestowed on the same temple by the four leaders of the local guild of 360 merchants.[1]

The examples mentioned above show that many Jaina monasteries were founded in Karnataka during the early medieval age. They also indicate how the solitary unsocial life of the Jaina monks was transformed into cenobite life which developed fully in Karnataka during the 12th-13th centuries.

In course of time the *maṭhavāsī* monks or those who lived permanently in monasteries came to be distinguished from the *vanavāsī* or the forest-dwelling monks. The wandering ascetics still emphasised the pristine purity of the monk's conduct. They retained their puritan and hermetical habits, living in forests and depending solely on pure alms for their sustenance.

The continued existence of the wandering ascetics is attested by Guṇabhadra and Somadeva, who flourished in Karnataka during the 9th-10th centuries. The *Yaśastilaka*[2] of Somadeva refers to a roving group of monks and nuns under the guidance of the sage Sudatta, who did not allow the Jaina monks to stay in the monasteries of Rājapura, for this would make them worldly. Guṇabhadra in his *Ātmānuśāsana* refers to the *vanavāsī* monks who were completely devoid of possessions.[3]

Though the two modes of monastic life existed side by side in Karnataka, settled life gained ascendency over the

1. *EI*, xiii, pp. 190ff.
2. *Yaśastilaka*, pt. i, BK i, p. 107.
3. A. N. Upadhye, (ed.), *Ātmānuśāsana*, v. 149, pp. 141-2.

wandering life. The settlement of monks in monasteries facilitated possession of vast economic resources including both movable and immovable property. They now erected and renovated the dilapidated Jaina monasteries, and added charity houses to them for the benefit of the Jaina ascetics as well as the sick and poor persons. The change in the conduct of the Jaina monks is clearly indicated by Indranandi. He refers in his *Nītisāra*[1] to the monks who renovated decaying Jaina *basadis*, provided food to the ascetics and distributed charity out of their wealth. It is evident that the Jaina monks frequently evaded the established rules against non-possession of property an essential prerequisite for the purity of the monk's life.

Other rules governing the conduct of the Jaina monks also became lax. All this is evident from the *Ātmānuśāsana* of Guṇabhadra. It laments the shortage of virtuous monks and complains against the vices that had crept in the monastic life of his time. It states that the monks unable to endure hardship sought resort in the villages just as a deer runs away from the forest at the sight of the lion at night.[2] Somadeva too in his *Yaśastilaka* notes the paucity of the monks of merit. Still he encourages the Jaina laity to revere them on the ground that they (the monks) are the incarnations of the ancient monks.[3] He advises the householders not to test the purity of monks for giving gift; the householders are purified by the mere act of giving donation.[4] All this would suggest degradation from the original standard of the monk's conduct in the monasteries. It was possibly the chief reason why Somadeva emphasised the mere act of making gifts rather than the purity of the monk's conduct.

The transition in the mode of monk's living produced certain important consequences. Permanent residence helped the organisation of the Jaina church in Karnataka into one compact unit during the early medieval age. It is thought

1. *Nītisāra*, vv. 48-50, cited in N.R. Premi, op. cit., p. 487.
2. A. N. Upadhye, (ed.), *Ātmānuśāsana*, v. 197.
3. *Yaśastilaka*, pt. ii, BK viii, p. 407.
4. Ibid.

that in the beginning of the Christian era the Digambaras had to live in a new region and face the new people; so they had to impress the people there more by their puritan behaviour than by organised monastic life.[1]

The creation, development and preservation of the sacred texts of the Jainas was a notable achievement of the new monastic life in Karnataka. Free from the worries of constant movements, the monks developed a sense of religious solidarity and devoted much time and energy to the study and exposition of the Jaina scriptures.

The rise of Kāvya and Purāṇic literature and the development of regional languages may be attributed to the Jaina monks and preceptors who lived in the monasteries. They mastered the various south Indian languages besides Sanskrit and Apabhraṁśa for the propagation of the Jaina faith among the people and enriched the different branches of learning such as philosophy, ethics, grammar, logic, mathematics, etc.

Pūjyapāda, who was the preceptor of the Gaṅga king Durvinīta, wrote several important Sanskrit works. The *Śabdāvatāra* on the *sūtras* of Pāṇini, the *Sarvārthasiddhi*, and the *Jainendra Vyākaraṇa* are all attributed to him. Ravisena, who composed the Jaina *Rāmāyaṇa* known as the *Padmapurāṇa*, flourished during the 6th-7th centuries. Besides, the Jaina ācāryas such as Vīrasena, Jinasena, Guṇabhadra and Somadeva cultivated Sanskrit with great vigour.

Akalaṅka, regarded as the founder of the medieval school of logic, was followed by Prabhācandra, Vidyānandi and Vādighangala Bhaṭṭa. The last one was well-versed in the three schools of logic and in the Lokāyata, Sāṅkhya, Vedānta and Bauddha systems of philosophy.[2] The period that covered the 9th-10th centuries, proved to be the most eventful in the growth of Kannaḍa literature. Pampa, Ponna and Ranna, the three literary gems of our period, made valuable contributions to Kannaḍa literature. The Jainas continued to

1. S.B. Deo, op. cit., p. 361.
2. *MAR*, 1921, pp. 23-4.

monopolise the Kannaḍa literature in the 11th-12th centuries. With the exception of one or two, all poets, from the beginning to the middle of the 12th century, were of the Jaina faith.[1] Among the eminent Kannaḍa poets, Śrīdharācārya, Karṇapārya and Nemicandra figured prominently in Jaina literature. Kanti, the earliest Jaina poetess in Kannaḍa, also belonged to the 12th century.[2]

Social basis of the Jaina Monasteries in Karnataka

Since the monks and nuns began to live in fixed abodes in the midst of lay communities, they entered into constant social intercourse with the lay votaries in Karnataka during early medieval times. The Jaina monasteries were socially organised in such a way as to cater to the needs of all the classes of the Jaina society not only through religious teachings but also advice on political matters. The Jaina epigraphs as well as the literary texts from Karnataka reveal that some of the Jaina teachers acted as preceptors or instructors to kings, princes, and feudal lords who ruled over different parts of Karnataka. Pūjyapāda, Jinasena, Guṇabhadra, Ajitasena-bhaṭṭāraka and Vādighangala Bhaṭṭa were some of the prominent Jaina teachers who took active interest in the day to day activities of the royal courts. Vādighangala Bhaṭṭa's advice to the Rāṣṭrakūṭa King Kṛṣṇa III enabled the latter to conquer all regions.[3] The *Nītivākyāmṛta* represents Somadeva as a political thinker who composed this work for the guidance of the kings of Karnataka just as Machiavelli wrote *The Prince* to guide the Italian monarchs. Both Jinasena and Somadeva recognised the system of caste and enjoined the Jaina laity to adhere to their hereditary occupations in order to safeguard the interest of the ruling class. In the 11th-12th centuries, the Jaina teachers showed equal interest in managing the affairs of the Kingdoms in Karnataka. Vardhamānadeva, for example, took prominent part in the administration of the Hoysaḷa kingdom during the time of Vinayāditya. Besides, Municandra, who is styled as Raṭṭa rāja-guru, gained

1. G.S. Halapa, "Literary History of Karnataka", *Studies in Indian History and Culture*, ed. Srinivas Ritti, pp. 467-76.
2. S.R. Sharma, op. cit., p. 101.
3. *MAR*, 1921, pp. 23-4.

eminence not only as an administrator but also as a military general who extended the territory of the Raṭṭas and established their authority on a firm footing.[1] Thus, the Jainas adopted the method and tactics of the Brāhmaṇas in order to maintain their social status at the royal courts.

The patronage of the ruling class in early medieval times transformed the Jaina faith from a mere tissue of teachings into a living force in Karnataka politics.[2] A large number of Jaina epigraphs show that the people belonging to the upper strata of the Jaina society made the maximum number of endowments either to some Jaina establishments or particular Jaina monks. The Kadambas, the Gaṅgas, the western Cālukyas, the Rāṣṭrakūṭas, the later western Cālukyas, and the Hoysaḷas championed the cause of Jainism in Karnataka during the 5th-12th centuries. They gave regular gifts for the upkeep of the Jaina monasteries and the benefit of the different sects of the Digambaras.

The class of nobility, consisting mainly of the feudatory vassals, provincial governors and the military generals stood next to kings in patronising the Jaina faith in Karnataka. The earliest example of such benefaction is furnished by the copper plate grant of the western Cālukya king Pulakeśin. It refers to Sāmiyāra, a feudatory of Pulakeśin, who built a Jaina temple in 489 in the city of Alaktanagara and gave certain lands to it.[3] Although instances of benefactions made by feudatories to the Jainas and their establishments are meagre during the 6th-7th centuries, their number is impressive during the 8th-12th centuries when every attempt was made by the feudal lords of Mysore to add to the strength of the Jaina dharma.[4] Cāki-Rāja, who is styled as an *adhirāja* of the entire Gaṅga maṇḍala in an inscription of the 9th century, was a feudatory of the Rāṣṭrakūṭa king Govinda III. He is said to have requested his lord to grant the village of Jālamaṅgala to a Jaina monk Arkakīrti as remuneration for removing the evil influence of Saturn from that of Vimalāditya, the Governor of Kunangil district.[5]

1. P. B. Desai, op. cit., p. 114.
2. B. A. Saletore, op. cit., p. 87.
3. *IA*, vii, no. xliv, pp. 209-15.
4. B.A. Saletore, op. cit., p. 87.
5. *EC*, xii, 61, Gb. pp. 30-1.

Among the Raṭṭa chiefs, the *mahāsāmanta* Pṛthvirāma appears to be a devout Jaina. He erected a Jaina temple at Saundatti in the Belgaum district of Mysore in the reign of Kṛṣṇa II and allotted eighteen *nivartanas* of land situated at four different places to it. He was a lay disciple of Indrakirtisvāmī of the Mailāpatīrtha and Kāreya gaṇa.[1] In 980 Śāntivarma, who served the Cālukya king of Kalyana, Taila II, gave one hundred and fifty *nivartanas* of land to the Jaina temple that he had built at Saundatti. His mother, Nijiyabbe, also granted one hundred and fifty *nivartanas* of cultivable land to the same Jaina temple.[2] The practice of extending patronage to Jaina establishments persisted among the princes of the Raṭṭa family in the 11th-12th centuries. In 1048 the *mahāsāmanta* Aṅka, who probably belonged to some other branch of the family than that of Pṛthvīrāma, made a gift of land to a Jaina temple.[3] Kārtavīrya II renewed the grant of land made by Pṛthvīrāma in the 10th century; his wife also made suitable provisions for the promotion of the Jaina faith.[4] In 1098 Kankakaira II, who was the elder brother of Kārtavīrya II, donated land to his teacher Kankaprabha Siddhāntadeva,[5] who was well-versed in the Jaina philosophy. Moreover, an epigraph from Saundatti, dated 1228,[6] described Lakṣmīdeva II as the disciple of the famous Jaina teacher Municandra, who took active interest in consolidating the Raṭṭa power in the 13th century.

Ladies belonging to the family of chiefs and nobles showed equal enthusiasm for the construction and upkeep of the Jaina monasteries. The most important of them was Kaṇḍācī, the wife of the feudatory chief Paramagūla, who lived during the reign of the Gaṅga king Śrīpuruṣa. In 776 she built the Lokatilaka Jinālaya which was endowed with the village Poṇṇalli included in the Nirgunda country.[7] Candi-

1. *JBBRAS*, x, pp. 194ff; *BKI*, iv, no. 13, p. 11.
2. Ibid, pp 204ff.
3. Ibid. x, pp. 172-3, cited in P.B. Desai, op. cit , p. 114.
4. Ibid.
5. *BKI*, iv, no. 62, p. 75.
6. *JBBRAS*, x, pp. 260ff.
7. *EC*, iv, Ng. 85, pp. 134-5.

yabbe,[1] another lady, gave a piece of land and 3 gold *gadyāṇas* to the *basadi* which she had built in Nandavara in the 10th century. Similar examples of women of the ruling class, who gained eminence for erecting *basadis* and maintaining them with endowments of land and village, are available from the 11th-12th centuries. In 1007 Attimabbe, the wife of the general Nāgadeva constructed a Jaina temple at Lakkuṇḍi in the Gadag taluq of the Dharwar district and endowed it with the gift of land. The gift was handed over to Arhanandi-Paṇḍita of the Surāṣṭra gaṇa and Kaurūr gaccha.[2] In about 1050 Poccabbarsi built a *basadi* and endowed it with land in 1058.[3] Malala Devī, wife of Kīrtideva constructed another Jaina temple in 1077 and granted the village Siḍḍaṇi in Kuppaṭūr.[4] Kāliyakka, the wife of an official of the western Cālukya king Tribhuvanamalla Deva, caused to be made a Jaina temple in Sambanur in the Davangere taluq of the Chitaldroog district in 1128 and gave a gift of land for the services of the god and for the maintenance of priests living there.[5] Epigraphic evidence from early medieval Karnataka may be adduced to prove that often such state officers as village-headmen, who figure in inscriptions as *gāvuṇḍas*, also made munificent endowments to the Jaina monasteries. An undated epigraph assigned to the middle of the 8th century registers a gift of land for the charity house attached to the Jaina monastery constructed by Dharmagāvuṇḍa. It also records a grant of wet land for the benefit of the same Jaina temple by Doṇagāvuṇḍa.[6] Nagamayya, son of the *gavuṇḍasvāmi* of Tairūr, built a stone temple of Jinendra and gave one *kaṇḍuga* of land for its maintenance in the 9th century.[7] In 933 Ballajja, the *gāvuṇḍa* of Kavujageri, donated land for the Jaina temples and *maṭhas* erected by him at Kavujageri and other places in the Ron taluq of the Dharwar district.[8] In 959 the *gāvuṇḍa*-

1. *SII,* ix, pt. i, no. 62, p. 35.
2. *BKI*, i, pt. i, no. 52, p. 39.
3. *EC*, ix, Cg. 35, 37, p. 173-4.
4. Ibid, viii, Sb. 262, pp. 41-2.
5. Ibid. xi, Dg. 90, pp 68-9.
6. *KI*, i, no. 3, pp 4-5.
7. *EC*, iii, Md. 13, p. 38.
8. *BKI*, i, pt. i, no. 35, p. 21.

svāmī Kalteyamma and others granted land and money for imparting education and the expenses of the Jaina monastery attached to the Jaina temple at Soratur in the same district. The gift was entrusted to the care of Bhimarāsi-bhaṭāra.[1] An epigraph from Koṇṇur dated 1087[2] refers to Nidhiyama gāvuṇḍa who erected a Jaina temple at Koṇḍanūru in the Gokak taluq of the Belgaum district and gave a gift of land to his teacher Śrīdharadeva, who belonged to the Balātkara-gaṇa of the Mūla saṅgha. Another record of 1160[3] registers the construction of a *basadi* by the Hoysaḷa gāvuṇḍa which was endowed with land obtained by the Hoysaḷa king. Similar attempts of temple construction were made by Biṭhigāvuṇḍa, who donated the village Madahaḷḷi for repairing the temple and performing worship therein in the last decade of the 12th century.[4]

The early Jaina records[5] from Karnataka do not furnish any information about the support of the mercantile people to Jaina religious institutions. The merchants seem to have appeared first in the donative records of the 10th century, when some merchant donors are said to have financed Jaina establishments. An inscription[6] from Mulgund in Dharwar district, dated 902-3, speaks of Cīkārya, son of Candrārya of the Vaiśya caste, as the founder of a local Jaina temple. Cīkāryas' son Arasārya also donated land for the maintenance of the establishment. It further registers gift of another piece of land to the same temple by the trading guilds of 360 merchants. Another record[7] of 950 refers to certain unnamed *saṭṭis* (merchants) who made an annual grant of fixed amount for the Jaina temple during the reign of the Śāntara king Jinadatta-Rāya. Except these two epigraphs, we do not come across any evidence of gifts and donations made by the merchants to the Jaina sanctuaries between the 5th and the

1. *BKI*, no. 39, p. 24.
2. *JBBRAS*, x, pp. 287ff
3. *EC*, vi, Md. 69, pp. 12-3.
4. Ibid. iv, Gu. 27, p, 40.
5. *Top. List of Inscriptions*, i, p. 265.
6. *EI*, xiii, pp. 190ff.
7. *EC*, vii, ch. 114, p, 37.

10th centuries.

The comparative paucity of evidence of the mercantile support to Jainism during the 5th-10th centuries may be attributed to the decline of trade and commerce which undermined the economic and social status of merchants during this period. It was not until the 10th century that the trade with the Arab and the Chinese world was revived, merchants reemerged as a dominant social group not only in Karnataka but also in the whole of South India.[1] Thus, they began to figure prominently in the donative records of the later western Cālukyas and the Hoysaḷas who ruled over Karnataka during the 11th-12th centuries. In addition to the decline of trade and commerce, the puritan practices of the Jainas also retarded the progress of Jainism among the commercial communities in Karnataka who found it difficult to follow its rigid religious observances in the early stages. As the Jainas became more lax in the observance of their monastic conduct and practices by the 9th-10th centuries, it was easy for them to embrace Jainism.

From the 11th century onwards, the number of benefactions by the mercantile class to Jaina establishments seems to have considerably increased in Karnataka. Of the various kinds of gifts made by merchants, donations of land and village seem to have been fairly common as can be gleaned from several donative records of our period. In a record of Humcca, dated 1062[2], Paṭṭanasvāmī Nokkayya Seṭṭi figures not only as the builder of a Jinālaya but also the donor of the village Molakere, which he had purchased from the Śāntara king at the cost of 100 *gadyāṇas*. Another record of 1069[3] refers to the pious work of Māṇika Seṭṭi, who is said to have built a Jaina *basadi* at Mattavāra and endowed it with rich gifts of land. The Hoysaḷa king Vinayāditya II also donated the income incurred from the paddy crops in the village of Nāḍali

1. For a detailed discussion of the revival of trade in about the 10th century, see, R.C. Mazumdar, (ed.), *The Struggle for Empire*, pp. 552-3; *Journal of Indian History*, xxxii (1954), 139-43; Appadorai, *Economic Conditions of Southern India*, ii, 483-518.
2. *EC*, viii, Nr. 58, pp. 153-4.
3. *MAR*, 1932, pp. 172-4

and built several houses near the *basadi*. In 1078[1] Māci Seṭṭi and his younger brother Kali Seṭṭi gave a gift of land together with customs dues for the maintenance of the Nakhara-Jainālaya at Śravaṇa-Beḷgoḷa. Similar endowment of land is referred to in a donative record of 1080[2] which records the construction of a Jaina temple in Shikarpur by Biṇeya Bammu Seṭṭi and registers a gift of land for its maintenance.

Apart from gifts of land and village, merchants are also recorded to have donated gold, oil-mills, gardens and money in cash for the benefit of Jaina sanctuaries. In 1059[3] Biraya Seṭṭi made a gift of gold for the Nagara Jinālaya at Dambal in the Dharwar district. In 1096[4] Sovi Seṭṭi gave a gift of garden to Cārukīrti-Paṇḍita of the Yāpanīya saṅgha at Doni in the same district. Nollabbi Seṭṭi donated two oil mills and gardens for the Trikūṭa Jinālaya in 1125.[5] Still another record of Śravaṇa-Beḷgoḷa, dated 1175 tells us that all the merchants of this holy place promised to pay annually certain dues on Coral to provide for flowers in the Jaina temples of Gommaṭadeva and Pārśvadeva. That the Karnataka merchants made lavish donations to Jaina religious institutions is amply proved by no less than ten examples of land and village endowments recorded in the 12th century epigraphs.[6]

Donative records of the merchants also indicate the growing authority of the trading communities over the religious bodies during the 12th-13th centuries. Thus in a record of 1195 the merchants of Śravaṇa-Beḷgoḷa are said to have been entrusted with the task of protecting the Nagara Jinālaya built by the Hoysaḷa minister Nāgadeva.[7] In the same record,

1. *EC*, xii, Tp. 101, pp 61-2.
2. Ibid. vii, Sk. 8, p. 39.
3. *BKI*, i, pt. i, no. 94, p. 89.
4. Ibid i, pt ii, no. 140, p. 169.
5. *EC*, ii, SB 241, p. 103.
6. *EC*, vii, Sh. 57, A D. 1115, p 23; *EC*, ii, SB 137, A D 1117, p. 64; *EC*, iv, Ng. 103, A.D. 1120, p 141; ibid iv, Kr. 3, A D. 1125, p. 99; *MAR*, 1930, p. 247; *KI*, i, pp. 63-4; *MAR*, 1943, p. 75; *EC*, v, Hn. 129, A.D. 1140, p. 36; ibid. v, Ak. 1, A.D 1169, pp. 112-3; ibid. iv, Ng. 70, A.D. 1178, p. 130.
7. *EC*, ii, SB 335, pp. 142 4.

the newly emergent merchant class traced their descent from the eminent lineage of Khaṇḍali and Mūlabhadra. It also proves their intense desire for gaining social status.[1]

From the above analysis of the social basis of Jaina monasteries it is clear that Jainism prevailed among all sections of Karnataka society during early medieval period. But the number of donors from the upper classes was greater than from the merchants and commoners.

Economic Aspects of the Jaina Monasteries in Karnataka

The material basis of the Jaina monasteries in Karnataka was provided by the generous benefactions, bestowed upon them by the princes and rich persons. Generally the villages and plots of land were made over to the Jaina monks and they formed the chief source of income of the Jaina monasteries. Such villages were declared to be tax-free. The beneficiaries were given the right to collect taxes and other dues, previously paid to the state treasury. These economic advantages became almost permanent because grants were usually renewed by the donors. The Kadamba Copper plates state that the Kadamba king Harivarmā perpetuated the grant of the village for feeding the Jaina ascetics and for the performance of the temple rituals, which Mṛgeśavarmā had built at Halsi in the Belgaum district in the 6th century.[2] In another record of 859 Naganandyācārya is said to have received the gift of land on behalf of the Nāgula *basadi* for his life time.[3]

In some cases the donors fixed the income derived from the benefactions, and the inhabitants were asked to pay it regularly to the donee. In the reign of the Gaṅga king Rācamalla II, twelve small villages of Biliyur in Peddoregare were donated to the Satyavākya Jaina temple and the revenues derived from these villages amounted to 80 *gadyāṇas* of gold and 800 measures of paddy. Śivanandi was given the right to collect them for meeting the expenses of the Jaina temple.[4] In

1. *EC*, ii, SB 335, pp. 142-4.
2. *IA*, vi, no. 25, p. 31.
3. *KI*, ii, no. 5, p. 16.
4. *EC*, i, Cg. 2, pp. 52-3.

968 the *mahāsāmanta* Paṇḍiga fixed the rent of the two villages at the rate of 50 *gadyāṇas*.[1] In the same century the Gaṅga king Mārasiṁha II gave the gift of the village named Bagiyūr and the income from it was fixed at the rate of 20 *gadyāṇas* in cash and 12 *kaṇḍugas* in grain.[2]

Cultivable fields, gardens, oilmills and the customs duties constituted another important source of income for the Jaina monasteries in Karnataka. As the donated fields were generally arable and wet lands, the monasteries earned considerable income from their cornfields and fruit gardens.

Inscriptions do not throw light on the actual tillers of the vast tracts of donated lands, owned by the Jaina monasteries. If Devasena, the author of *Darśanasāra*, is to be believed, a section of the Jaina monks, belonging to the Draviḍa-saṅgha, engaged themselves in cultivation. He states that Vajranandī, the founder of the saṅgha. accummulated great demerits by cultivating the land and carrying on mercantile activities to earn livelihood.[3]

But in general the Jaina monks did not follow this practice. Generally the monks had nothing to do directly with cultivation. Possibly they got the land cultivated through peasants on the basis of lease or sharecropping or overseers and agricultural labourers may have been employed for looking after the lands under the direct cultivation of the Jaina establishments.

Very scanty evidence is available to find out the actual share of the produce collected by the monks from their tenants. From a record of the 9th century it can be inferred that the Jaina beneficiary was empowered to collect 1/10 of the produce of Padeyūr.[4] But we cannot say whether this practice prevailed in all parts of Mysore in the period under our study.

The safety and preservation of the economic rights were

1. *EC*, xi, Cd. 74, p. 16.
2 *MAR*, 1921, pp. 23-4.
3. N.R. Premi, (ed.), *Darśanasāra*, vv. 24-7, pp. 12-3.
4. *EC*. ix, NL 61, pp. 44-5.

guaranteed by the donors under moral threats. The alienation of the donated land is held as heinous crime for the Jainas in the imprecatory verses of the records. The person who confiscates the grant through greed or impiety is declared to be guilty of the five great sins.[1] The property of the gods is called dreadful poison, for it is considered capable of destroying not only the seizer but also his sons and grandsons.[2] Moreover, the monks themselves took the task of defending the monasteries and their huge wealth from the aggressors. A record of the 10th century tells us about Moni-bhaṭāra, a disciple of Guṇacandra-bhaṭāra, who protected the Jaina monastery of Kellangere at the cost of his life,[3] when Ballapa tried to capture it in the reign of the Gaṅga king Būtuga.

The Jaina monks enjoyed not only fiscal but also administrative rights over the lands assigned to the monasteries. An epigraph of the 10th century speaks[4] of the administration of the village Pasuṇḍi or modern Asundi in the Gadag taluq of the Dharwar district by the preceptor, Candraprabha-bhaṭāra, the high priest of Dhora-Jinālaya at Bankapur. The village evidently came as an endowment to the Jaina temple. Another record of the same century refers to Śrīvara-Matisāgara-Paṇḍita as the ruler of Śravaṇa-Beḷgoḷa, which was the chief centre of the Jaina monastic organisations.[5] Though the early records are silent about the grant of the administrative rights, it was difficult to enforce fiscal rights without some measure of administrative authority. It seems that the monasteries were equally free from royal interference in matters of administration at least from the 10th century. For the maintenance of law and order in the area assigned to them, they may have depended upon the kings.

Inscriptions show that the monks, who were the custodians of the Jaina monasteries, wielded considerable control

1. *IA*, vii, nos. 35-6.
2. *EC*, i, Cg 1, p. 51.
3. Ibid, v, BL 123, p. 80.
4. *BKI*, i, pt. i, no. 34, p. 20, cited in P.B. Desai, op. cit., p. 139.
5. *EC*, iii, Sr. 148, p. 34.

over the lands granted to the Jaina institutions. We have instances to show that they alienated land in favour of some other religious establishments or secular persons. Śrīnandi Paṇḍita is said to have granted some plots of land to his lay disciple Singaya who earmarked it for the purpose of providing food for the Jaina ascetics of Gudigere. We also learn that Śrīnandi-Paṇḍita gave one hundred and eleven *mattars* of rent-free land to the twelve *gāvuṇḍas*, and fifteen *mattars* of land to Rudrayya, the son of the Pergade Prabhākara, as a *sarvanamasya* grant to a Jaina temple of Śāntinātha which had been built by Someśvara II.[1]

The monks, who were granted huge land for enjoyment and maintenance of the Jaina monasteries, emerged as a land owning class in Karnataka during early medieval times. As they did not cultivate the land themselves but got it cultivated by their tenants, they may be regarded as the landed intermediaries between the donors and the real cultivators. Moreover, since the donee was empowered to alienate land in favour of secular persons, this gave rise to sub-infeudation which undermined the position of the actual tillers of the soil. Thus, we notice a few traits of the feudal system in the Jaina monastic organisation during the period under review. Professor R. S. Sharma[2] has suggested that with grants of land free from royal interference, the Buddhist temples and monasteries grew into later *maṭhas* which assumed a feudal character. We observe some feudal tendencies even in the land and village grants made to the Jaina monasteries which enjoyed full freedom from royal interference.

Proliferation of Monastic Orders

The proliferation of the monastic organisations in early medieval Karnataka is evident from the contemporary Jaina epigraphs. The monastic order, referred to in the early records of the Gaṅgas and the Kadambas, was evidently the Mūla saṅgha. An inscription of 370[3] refers only to the Mūla saṅgha

1. *IA*, viii, pp. 36-7.
2. R.S. Sharma, *Light on Early Indian Society and Economy*, p. 150.
3. *EC*, x, ML 73, p. 172.

and in another record of 425[1] Candranandī and other monks are said to have belonged to the same monastic order. But later records use such terms as the saṅgha, gaṇa and gaccha to indicate the monastic orders of the Digambaras.

Anvaya is first met with in a fifth century inscription which refers to Kundakundānvaya.[2] The records of the 7th-8th centuries are replete with references to gaṇa. A Śravaṇa-Beḷgoḷa record of the 8th century mentions Aji-gaṇa of the Nimilūr Saṅgha.[3] Mention is also made of Devagaṇa[4] and Paralūra gaṇa[5] in the epigraphs of the western Cālukya kings during the same century. Similarly, the term *gaccha* which appears in a copper plate grant of Śrīpuruṣa in the 8th century, refers to Eregittūrgaṇa and Pulikalgaccha.[6]

The multiplication of the monastic orders is also apparent from the fact that several terms are used to explain the position of a particular order in the monastic gradations. In the 8th century, an inscription refers to three divisions of the monastic orders such as the Nandi saṅgha, Eregittūr gaṇa and Pulikal gaccha.[7] In the 9th century, the Mūla Saṅgha had its subdivisions named Deśīya gaṇa and Pustaka gaccha.[8] The Pogariya gaṇa is mentioned as a branch of the Sena-anvaya, subdivisions of the Mūlasaṅgha in the same century.[9] The epigraphs of the 10th century also refer to the hierarchical gradations of the monastic orders. The Draviḍa Saṅgha, for example, consisted of Kundakundānvaya and Pustaka gaccha during the 10th century.[10] Further subdivisions into four or five grades are referred to in later epigraphs. An epigraph of 1098 refers to as many as four gradations of the monastic

1. *EC*, xv, ML 73, p. 172.
2. Ibid. i, Cg 1, p. 51.
3. Ibid. ii, SB 97, p. 43.
4. *BKI*, iv, no. 7, p. 7.
5. Ibid. no. 9, p. 9; *KI*, i, no. 3, pp. 4-5.
6. *EC*, iv, Ng 85, pp. 134-5.
7. Ibid. Ng 85, pp. 134-5.
8. *EI*, vi, p. 36.
9. Ibid. x, pp. 65 ff.
10. *EC*, vi, Md 11, p. 60.

order such as the Mūla Saṅgha, Deśīya gaṇa, Pustaka gaccha and Piriyasamudāya.[1]

The monastic orders mentioned above suffered from internal bickerings, which first appeared in the Mūla Saṅgha, the oldest monastic order of the Digambara monks. This united original order first split into two permanent sects, the Digambaras who remained completely nude and the Śvetāmbaras who put on white cloth to cover nudity in the first-second centuries. The presence of the Śvetāmbaras is attested by the Kadamba Copper Plates of the 5th century. They obtained considerable success in proselytizing the south Indian people in the beginning but subsequently lagged behind the Digambaras and almost vanished from the scene.[2]

The Digambara monastic order figured prominently in the history of the Jaina Church of south India. They first appeared in an inscribed record of the 4th century.[3] Candranandī and other monks of the Śrī Mūla Saṅgha are again mentioned in an another inscription of the 5th century.[4] Kundakundānvaya,[5] which is met in an epigraph of the same century, was possibly the synonym of the Mūla Saṅgha. It was named after the famous Jaina teacher Kundakunda, who flourished in the south during the early years of the Christian era.

The Yāpanīya Saṅgha which was another important monastic order, next to the Mūla Saṅgha, flourished in the northern and southern parts of Karnataka. It had much in common with both the Digambaras and the Śvetāmbaras, and its teachers played a distinguished role in propagating the Jaina faith in south India and influencing its monastic traditions. The influence was exercised from Karnataka, which was the main sphere of the Yāpanīya activities. Excepting one or two stray references to their existence in the Telgu country,

1. P.B. Desai, op. cit., p. 247.
2. Ibid. p. 98.
3. *EC*, x, ML 73, pp. 172-3.
4. *Ibid.* ML 72, p. 172.
5. Ibid. i, Cg 1, p. 51.

the Yāpanīyas are not met with in other parts of south India.[1] This is clearly proved by the Kadamba records of the 5th-6th centuries. They show that Palāśika or modern Halsi in the Belgaum district was the chief stronghold of this order. At this place lived also the Nirgranthas and the Kūrcakas,[2] but the Yāpanīyas were possibly more important. Ravivarmā donated land for providing food to the Yāpanīya ascetics during the four months of the rainy season.[3] Devavarmā, another king of the Kadamba dynasty, also gave land at Siddakedara to them.[4] Ravikīrti belonged to the Yāpanīya Saṅgha[5] and constructed a Jaina temple at Aihoḷe in the Bijapur district in the 7th century.[6] All this indicates the increasing importance of the Yāpanīya order in the kingdom of the western Cālukya kings.

The monks of the Yāpanīya order are seen active at Śilāgrāma to the west of Mānyapura in the Gubbi taluq of the Tumkur district in the first quarter of the 9th century in the reign of the Rāṣṭrakūṭa king Govinda III.[7] As the epigraph refers to Arkakīrti, a well known monk of the Yāpanīya Nandi saṅgha and Punnagavṛkṣamūlagaṇa, the order started in the Rāṣṭrakūṭa kingdom in the middle of the 8th century. This epigraph also shows the monastic subdivisions of the Yāpanīya Saṅgha. A record of the 10th century, which has been found at Saundatti in the Belgaum district, refers to Indrakīrti and other monks as belonging to the Kāreya gaṇa.[8] In another epigraph of the same century, Bāhubali-bhaṭṭāraka is said to have belonged to the Kaṇḍūr gaṇa.[9] Both the Kāreya gaṇa and the Kaṇḍūr gaṇa formed branches of the Yāpanīya Saṅgha during early medieval times. Evidently the Yāpanīya Saṅgha exercised great influence upon the Jainas of Karnataka, and

1. P.B. Desai, op. cit., p. 98.
2. *IA*, vi, no. 21, p. 25.
3. Ibid, no. 22, p. 27.
4. Ibid. vii, no, 35, pp. 34-5.
5. *JBU*, (May, 1933), p. 233.
6. *IA*, viii, pp. 237-45; *EI*, vi, p. 12.
7. *EC*, xii, Gb 61, pp. 30-1.
8. *JBBRAS*, x, pp. 194 ff.
9. Ibid. pp. 204 ff.

it developed several important centres such as the Halsi and Saundatti in the Belgaum district, Aihoḷe in the Bijapur district and Śilāgrāma in the Tumkur district of Mysore. Some other Jaina records from Karnataka reveal an interesting information about the role of the Yāpanīyas who concentrated their religious activities in the region around Dharwar, Kolhapur and Sedam in the Gulbaraga district during the 11th-12th centuries. They did pioneer work for popularising the worship of the mother goddesses in Karnataka. Jayakīrtideva of the Yāpanīya Saṅgha is recorded to have built a temple for the Jaina goddess Jvālāmālinī at Jāvur in the Navalgund taluq of the Dharwar district.[1] Besides Jāvur, Doṇi, Hoṇṇur and Sedam were other important seats of the Yāpanīya sect. In 1079 Sovisetṭi constructed a Jaina temple at Doṇi in the Dharwar district and endowed it with a gift of land. Cārukīrti-Paṇḍita of the Yāpanīya Saṅgha received the gift.[2] In 1110 Bammagāvuṇḍa erected another Jaina *basadi* at Hoṇṇur in the Kolhapur region, who belonged to the Punnagavṛkṣamūlagaṇa, a branch of the Yāpanīya Saṅgha.[3] From the above records it is clear that the monks of the Yāpanīya Saṅgha contributed much to the growth of tantric practices in Karnataka during early medieval times.

The epigraphs of the 8th and the 10th centuries show that several new monastic orders were formed in the Hassan and Banglore districts of Mysore. The inscriptions at Śravaṇa-Beḷgoḷa refer to the existence of four monastic orders such as the Navilūr, Kittūr, Kolaṭṭūr and Malanur Saṅgha in the 8th century. All these orders seem to have derived their names from the places where they originated. Thus, we notice territorial influence upon the formation of the Jaina Saṅgha in Karnataka in early medieval times. These monastic orders may have been the result of personal zeal of the Jaina monks who lived and practised the faith at those places. They were perhaps the descendants of the early preceptors such as Prabhā-

1. P.B. Desai, op. cit., p. 143.
2. Ibid. p. 144.
3. Ibid. p. 119.

candra[1] and Ariṣṭanemi,[2] who performed religious suicide on the summit of Candragiri hill at Śravaṇa-Beḷgoḷa in the 7th century. After the death of the teachers the disciples probably founded new monastic orders at different places.

Of four monastic orders mentioned above, the Navilūr Saṅgha was known by different names such as the Namilūr[3] and Nimilūr[4] Saṅgha. The Mayūrgrāma Saṅgha,[5] which appears in an inscription of the 8th century, may also be identified with the Namalūr Saṅgha, because the same inscription refers to the nun Prabhāvatī of the fortunate Namilūr Saṅgha and Damitāmatī of the Mayūrgrāma Saṅgha,[6] and both are stated to have performed the religious rite known as the *sallekhanā* at the same place. The other monastic order was the Kittūr Saṅgha.[7] Rice has identified Kittūr with Kīrtipura, the capital of Punnāḍ 10,000 in the 3rd century.[8] Its present site is modern Kittur, which lay to the south of the present Mysore state. The Kolaṭṭūr Saṅgha,[9] which is the third monastic order, remains unidentified so far. The Malanur-Saṅgha,[10] founded in the 8th century, was possibly connected with the Draviḍa Saṅgha, because it is described as a branch of the Senagaṇa and Draviḍa-Saṅgha in a record of the 11th century.[11]

Besides the above-mentioned ascetic orders of the Digambara monks, the Draviḍa Saṅgha deserves special mention, for it played an important role in advancing the new monasticism in Karnataka. Its origin and date, owing to the contradictory references in literary texts and inscriptions, have been so far under debate. Devasena in his *Darśanasāra* states

1. *EC*, ii, SBI, p. 1.
2. Ibid. SB. 11, p. 4.
3. Ibid. SB 109, p. 45; ibid. SB 114, pp. 45-6.
4. Ibid. SB 97, p. 43.
5. Ibid. SB 108, p. 45.
6. Ibid. SB 114, p. 45.
7. Ibid. SB 81, p. 41.
8. Lewis Rice, *Mysore Gazetteer*, ii, p. 223.
9. *EC*, ii, SB 92, 93 and 96, p. 43.
10. Ibid. SB 25, p. 6.
11. P.B. Desai, op. cit., p. 221.

that it was founded by Vajranandī, a disciple of Pūjyapāda, at Madura in the Vikram era 526 which corresponds to 469.[1] But on the basis of the epigraphic evidence Saletore concludes that the Draviḍa Saṅgha at Madura was set up by Vajranandī in the last quarter of the 9th century or in the first quarter of the 10th century.[2] Desai also associates the Draviḍa-Saṅgha with the Tamil country. He cites an inscription from Śravaṇa-Beḷgoḷa dated 700, which refers to Paṭṭini-Gurvaḍigal, who observed the vow of *sallekhanā* on the Candragiri hill. He analyses the term Paṭṭini as a Tamil expression which is commonly met in the inscriptions of the Tamil country.[3] But the view that the Draviḍa Saṅgha originated in Tamil Nadu is hardly convincing because we get hardly a reference to this sect in the inscriptions of the Tamil country. On the other hand, numerous inscriptions from Karnataka speak of its existence in the Kannaḍa country. On account of its connection with the Kannaḍa region, R. N. Nandi[4] rightly rejects the above-mentioned view and states that the Draviḍa Saṅgha originated and flourished in Karnataka during early medieval times. He bases his opinion on the study of the *Jvālinīkalpa*, which was composed by Indranandi in 939 Indranandi who belonged to the Draviḍa Saṅgha, mentions five generations of preceptors from Helācārya, the head of the Draviḍa Saṅgha. Counting 25 years for each generation Helācārya can be placed in the first quarter of the 9th century, when the order was founded by Vajranandī. The text also refers to Nīlagiri near Hemagrāma n Mysore where Helācārya propitiated Jvālāmālinī.[5] The description of the Draviḍa Saṅgha as a subdivision of the Mūla Saṅgha also shows that the order originated in Mysore and belonged to the Jainas of Mysore. In 1040 the sect is characterized as a branch of the Mūla Saṅgha. It is also referred to as a subsect of the Kundakundānvaya.[6]

1. N.R. Premi, (ed.), *Darśanasāra*, v. 28, p. 13.
2. B.A. Saletore, op. cit., p. 238.
3. P.B. Desai, op. cit., p. 222.
4. R.N. Nandi, *Religious Institutions and cults in the Deccan*, pp. 62.
5. Ibid.
6. Ibid.

The Deśīgaṇa, variously known as Deśīya, Deśīga and Deśīka in the epigraphs from Śravaṇa-Beḷgoḷa and other places, emerged as an important monastic order of the Digambara monks. An epigraph of 860[1] describes Trikālayogīśa as belonging to the Pustaka gaccha, Deśīya gaṇa of the Mūla Saṅgha. Further references are found in the records of the 10th-11th centuries. The Pustaka gaccha, which was an important branch of this order, is referred to in the inscriptions of our period. Govind Pai states that the country between the western Ghats, the Karnataka country of ancient and medieval times and the Godavari river was known as *deśa* and the members of the Nandi-saṅgha who settled in this area called their order as the Deśī gaṇa,[2] Clearly the word deśī is derived from the Sanskrit deśa which means homeland. Possibly the monks of this order belonged to the native Digambara Church of the south, for it is frequently referred to as a branch of the Mūla saṅgha or Kundakundānvaya, which was the oldest monastic order in Karnataka.

Divergent doctrines and rituals led to differences between the monks and caused the proliferation of the Digambara ascetic orders. The followers of the Yāpanīya Saṅgha, which won wide popularity in Karnataka during the period under review, developed their own theology. Contrary to the opinion of the Digambaras, they advocated salvation for women, householders and even the followers of the other faiths. They put on white dress as against the Digambara practice of nudity. The liberal attitude of the Yāpanīyas towards women made this sect popular with women in Karnataka. They were the early pioneers of the reformation movement in the Jaina Church of south India, and their example and precept might have been followed and assimilated by the teachers of several other monastic orders in Karnataka[3] during early medieval times.

The foundation of the Draviḍa Saṅgha during the early part of the 9th century was also the result of the

1. *EI*, vi, p. 36.
2. *JA*, i, no. 2, pp. 65 ff.
3. P.B. Desai, op. cit., p. 167.

transgression of the old ascetic practices. Vajranandī, the founder of this Saṅgha, demanded considerable degree of latitude in matters relating to habitation and dietary practices. He allowed his followers to take anything that they liked, to bathe in cold water and to take food in any position against the prevailing rule of taking food in standing position.[1] Kumarāsena, who founded the Kāṣṭhā Saṅgha was expelled from his original Saṅgha because he discredited the Jaina practice of keeping the peacock feather's broom and instead of it allowed a broom made of the cow's tail.[2]

Rivalry among the Jaina monks possibly for the pontifical seat, which occupied the supreme position in the monastic organisation, also proved detrimental for the unity of the Jaina Saṅgha. Kumarāsena probably failed to secure the pontifical throne which passed to his colleague Jinasena, and hence he defected from the parent organisation Sena saṅgha to found a new order. In some cases, the personality of the Jaina teachers was also responsible for the creation of the monastic section. We may take the example of the Senagaṇa or the Senānvaya which became prominent in Mysore in the 9th century. It was originally known as the Pañcastūpānvaya. On account of the eminence attained by Vīrasena and Jinasena, the original Pañcastūpānvaya was replaced by the Senānvaya. In the *Dhavala*, Vīrasena describes himself as a member of the Pañcastūpānvaya while in *Jayadhavala*, Jinasena identifies himself as a member of this sect.[3]

The Order of Nuns and their Position

Nuns became the members of the Jaina monastic community since its foundation, and like monks they renounced the world for the attainment of spiritual liberation. The *Ratnakaraṇḍa-śrāvakācāra*,[4] which was composed in the first-second centuries, also refers to the order of nuns. It refers to the term *ajji* or *āryikā* which means a Jaina nun, who prepared herself for adopting the life of asceticism in the eleventh stage

1. N.R. Premi, (ed.), *Darśanasāra*, vv. 24-8, pp. 12-3.
2. Ibid. v. 34, p. 16.
3. N.R. Premi, op. cit , p. 127.
4. *Ratnakaraṇḍa-śrāvakācāra*, pt. i, p. 147.

of the householder's life. The *Varāṅgacarita*, which was composed by Jaṭāsiṁhanandi in the 7th century, informs us that several queens of Varāṅga took to the life of a nun.[1] They first paid homage to their preceptor and then went to a lonely place where they discarded their costly ornaments and dresses with the exception of a white *sārī* (garment for a woman) to cover nudity. They removed their hair at the time of initiation ceremony.[2]

The term, *ajji* or *āryikā* which stands for nuns, is frequently referred to in the Jaina epigraphs of our period. They denote probably the ordinary class of nuns. Inscriptions also refer to the term *kanti* or *ganti* which indicates a special class of nuns with higher position in the monastic organisation.[3] An inscription at Śravaṇa-Beḷgoḷa refers to the nun Rajñimatī-ganti of the illustrious Nimilār Saṅgha who lived in the 8th century.[4] Similar other records commemorate the death of the nuns Anantamatī-gantī,[5] Guṇamatī-avve,[6] Prabhāvatī and Damitāmatī[7] in the same century. This leaves no room for doubt about the existence of the order of nuns in Karnatka the early medieval age.

However, the nuns did not occupy any significant position in early monasticism. They were considered inferior to the monks. It is evident from the *Mūlācāra*[8] which states that a newly initiated monk was superior to a nun who practised the life of a nun for a long time. She was expected to pay respect to a monk or to a teacher by folding her knees and placing them on the ground.

Although the subordination of nuns to the monks persisted in the early medieval age, they were associated with the internal administration of the Jaina Church. Each order of

1. *Varāṅgacarita*, ch. 29, vv. 93-4, p. 292.
2. Ibid. ch. 30, v. 2, p. 293.
3. P.B. Desai, op. cit., p. 168.
4. *EC*, ii, SB 97, p. 43.
5. Ibid. SB 98, p. 43.
6. Ibid. SB 112, p. 45.
7. Ibid. SB 114, p. 45.
8. *Mūlācāra*, 10 : 18; cited in S.B. Deo, op. cit., p. 500.

nun was placed under the supervision of a preceptress who in her turn, was under the control of the chief pontiff. The *Varāṅgacarita*, which reflected the inferior position of the order of nuns, refers to the Jaina saṅgha under the control of the sage Varadatta. He is said to have directed the chief nun for giving instructions to the novices. She could not initiate a new lady into the order.[1]

Inscriptions do not give evidence of any independent monastic establishment exclusively meant for nuns. The establishment housed both monks and nuns. No grants of land and village were made only for the benefit of nuns. In an inscription from Arasibīḍi in the Belguam district, dated 1047, Akkādevī made a gift of land for the benefit of Goṇaḍa Beḍāṅgi Jinālaya and for the maintenance of the Ṛṣis and Ajjis, i.e., the Jaina monks and nuns, attached to this religious establishment.[2]

The internal administration of the order of nuns was carried on not by the monks but by the nuns themselves. In 1071[3] the nun Huliyabbājjike, who was the disciple of Śrīnandi-Paṇḍita of the Suraṣtha Gaṇa and Citrakūṭānvaya, received an endowment of land for managing the affairs of the Jaina sanctuary at Soraṭūr in the Dharwar district. She was evidently in charge of this Jaina temple and acted as the superintending priestess. In 1076 Aṣṭopavāsikantiyar, another nun, is said to have endowed land for the benefit of the Jaina temple of Pārśvanātha at Guḍigere.[4]

The increasing influence of the Jaina nuns is also shown by the fact that they entertained men as their disciples. Paṭṭinigurvaḍigal, mentioned in one inscription of Śravaṇa-Beḷgoḷa, was the preceptress of Ugrasena-guravaḍigal.[5] Arahānandi of the Valahāri Gaṇa was another monk who accepted discipleship of the nun Ayyopoti.[6] Desai traces the continuation of

1. *Varāṅgacarita*, ch. 31, vv. 6ff, p. 301.
2. *EI*, xvii, p. 122, cited by P.B. Desai, op. cit., p. 106.
3. *BKI*, i, pt., i, no. 111, p. 108.
4. *IA*, xviii, pp. 35ff.
5. *EC*, ii, SB 25, p. 6.
6. *EI*, vii, no. 25, pp. 177ff.

this practice even in the 12th century. On the basis of an undated inscription, assigned to 1110, he refers to the nun Rātrimatī of the Punnāgavṛkṣamūla Gaṇa of the Mūla Saṅgha, who acted as the preceptress of the male devotee Bammagāvuṇḍa.[1] These striking examples of nuns having monks as their disciples clearly demonstrate the persistence of matriarchal traditions of the peninsular India, which affected the Jaina monastic order in Karnataka during the early medieval period. Some other elements of matriarchal society such as the economic independence of women, worship of female deities or female ancestors, women's education on similar lines with males,[2] etc., are clearly perceived among the Jaina community in Karnataka. In Karnataka Jainism, women enjoyed religious privileges almost equal to those of men The religious independence given to Jaina women had its repurcussions in other spheres of Karnataka society. There is epigraphic evidence to show that a Jaina woman named Jakkiyabbe successfully discharged administrative duties in the Nagarakhaṇḍa 70 during the reign of the Rāṣṭrakūṭa king Kṛṣṇa III. We have also some Jaina women who distinguished themselves in the literary circle. Kanti, who belonged to the 12th century, figures eminently as the earliest Jaina poetess in the Kannaḍa literature. Besides, the adoration of female deities or female ancestors, which has been considered to be one of the elements of matriarchal survivals, is also proved by the worship of the Jaina goddesses in Karnataka during the 10th-12th centuries.

Church Administration and Its Functions

The emergence of the Jaina monasteries, separate from the temples, in Karnataka called for a system of discipline and organization, which could regulate the settled life of the Jaina monks and nuns. Therefore the Jainas evolved a well-regulated hierarchy of Church officers. They were the *ācārya* or the chief pontiff, the *upādhyāya* or the preceptor, the *gaṇadhara* or the head of a gaṇa and the *Sādhu* or the ordinary monk.

1. P.B. Desai, op. cit., p. 119.
2. Baron Omar Rolf Ehrenfels, *Mother-Right in India*, p. 11.

The chief pontiff stood at the head of the monastic organisation and received gift of land and villages. He was responsible for the observance of proper monastic conduct. He was the only person who initiated the novices into the order and gave instructions to the preceptor to guide them in the practice of monastic conduct. He also looked after the charity houses and received lands for their maintenance.[1] As the custodian of lands and villages for providing food to the Jaina ascetics,[2] he commanded absolute authority over other monks who depended on him for their sustenance.

The *ācārya* administered not only the Jaina monasteries but also the temples, usually attached to them in Karnataka. For the smooth running of the temple administration and the management of its huge property, two or more temples were grouped together, less prominent of them being attached to the big monastic establishment. An epigraph of the 10th century[3] throws sufficient light on this development. Candraprabha-bhaṭāra of the Dhora-Jinālaya of Bankapur was entrusted with the task of administering the Jaina temple of Pasuṇḍi or modern Asundi in the Dharwar district. Again, an epigraph of the Cālukya king Taila II, dated 992, registers the gift of lands to the five *maṭhas*, which were placed under the supervision of the *sthānādhipati* Gaṇadharadeva.[4] In 1080 Divakaranandi-Siddhāntadeva of the Kundakundānvaya and Pustakagaccha is recorded as the head of all the *basadis* of the Caṅgāḷva-tīrtha at Panasoge or modern Hanasoge in the Yedatore taluq of the Mysore district.[5]

Though the chief pontiff enjoyed full freedom from external secular authority, in some cases the Church administration was placed under the control of a committee or a trustee which put a check on the exercise of his absolute authority. A record of 1076[6] tells us that Singaya, a lay

1. *BKI*, IV, no. 4, p. 3 ; ibid. nos. 6 and 7, pp. 6-7.
2. *Top. List of Inscriptions*, i, p. 265 ; IA, VI, no. 25, p. 31.
3. BKI, I. pt. I, no. 34, p. 20.
4. *SII*. IX, pt. I, no. 77, p. 47.
5. *EC*, IV, Yd. 23, p. 55.
6. *IA*, XVIII, pp. 36ff.

disciple of Śrīnandi-Paṇḍita, gave land for providing food to the Jaina ascetics of Guḍigere. The epigraph explicitly enjoins the king, the paṇḍita and the twelve *gāvuṇḍas* to see that the proceeds of the land were used for that purpose.

The Jaina monasteries had also to discharge some social and economic functions for the regulation of the collective life of the monks and nuns in monasteries and the welfare of the Jaina community. The maintenance of the monasteries was a very important function. In most cases the donors showed concern for the proper upkeep of these religious establishments. It included repairing and restoration of the old and dilapidated *basadis* and *maṭhas*,[1] carrying out new works of construction[2] and the performance of the worship rituals therein. The term, *bhagna-saṁskāra* or *bhagna-kriyā*, which appears in the records of the Kadamba kings,[3] clearly indicates that the monasteries had to be kept in a good state. A record of the Kadamba king Mṛgeśavarmā registers the gift of land for sweeping out the Jaina temples.[4] Obviously the monasteries employed sweepers and scavengers.

Regular supply of food for the Jaina monks as well as the sick, poor and destitutes, was another important function of the Jaina monasteries. The Kadamba copper plates of the middle of the 5th-6th centuries speak of the provision of food in the monasteries. They show that the donor took special care to provide food for the ascetics of different Digambara sects such as the Yāpanīyas, the Nirgranthas and the Kūrcakas.[5] Another record registers the donation of the village Vasantavāṭaka for feeding the whole sect of the Digambara monks.[6] Candrakṣānta was the donee who had to manage the distribution of food among the Jainas. The Jaina practice of providing food to the Jaina ascetics as well as the poor persons continued in subsequent centuries. The Mulgund record of

1. *IA*. VII, nos. 35, 36, pp. 34-6 ; *EC*, IV, Ng 85, pp. 134-5 ; *BKI*, I, pt. I; no. 78, p. 68.
2. *EC*, IV, Ng 85. pp. 134-5.
3. *IA*. VII, nos. 36-7, pp. 36ff.
4. Ibid.
5. *IA*, vi. nos. 21-2, pp. 25-7.
6. Ibid. no, 25, p. 31.

Someśvara I, dated 1059, refers to the regular supply of food to the Jainas in the 11th century.[1] Bramma-Devarasa, a general of the Cālukya king also made a gift of the village for offering food to the Jaina monks in 1077.[2] Another epigraph of 1145 refers to the erection of a Jaina temple by Deva-Rāja, who was a minister of the Hoysaḷa king Viṣṇuvardhana. The king rewarded him for this meritorious work by donating land for performing worship and for free distribution of food in that Jaina temple.[3] But the Nañjedevaraguḍḍa stone inscription found in Somepur in the Hassan district gives us the most interesting details about the management of food distribution in the Abhinava Śāntideva Jaina temple in Dorasamudra. The Hoysaḷa king being pleased to see the conduct of free distribution of food in this temple made a gift of two villages to his guru Vajranandi Siddhāntadeva in order to carry on this work in 1192.[4] From these records it is apparent that the Jaina *maṭhas* regularly fed the monks, who either stayed in the monasteries or paid occasional visits to it during early medieval times.

The Jaina monasteries also rendered valuable services to the cause of education in Karnataka. Epigraphic sources frequently refer to the donation of lands and villages for imparting education[5] in the early medieval age. The gifts were known as the *Vidyā-dāna* or gifts of learning. Thus, the Jaina monasteries in Karnataka were living institutions for learning, where pupils were taught the various branches of knowledge. The academic pursuits of the Jaina teachers contributed to the development of Jaina literature. The Jaina literature of the 9th and the 10th centuries owed its creation and development to various Jaina monasteries in Karnataka.

Moreover, the Jaina monasteries appeared to be the pioneers in the work of charity. Elaborate provisions were made for the maintenance of *dāna-śālā* or charity houses, which were

1. *EI*, xvi, p. 57.
2. *EC*, vii, Sk. 124, p. 96.
3. Ibid. iv, Ng. 76, pp. 131-2.
4. *MAR*, 1926, pp. 50-2.
5. *EC*, v, Ag. 24, p. 250 ; *BKI*, i pt i, no. 39, p. 24 ; *SII*. ix. pt. i, no. 67, pp. 38-9 ; ibid. no. 117, p. 92 ; *EC*, iv. Ng. 20, p. 116.

attached to the Jaina maṭhas. In 683 the western Cālukya king Vinayāditya gave the gift of a village for maintaining the charity house attached to the Śaṅkha-Jinendra temple at Lakshamesvara in the Dharwar district.[1] Similar grants of land and village[2] were made by other kings of the same dynasty in the 8th century. Guṇacandrapaṇḍitādeva of the Kunda-kundānvaya and Deśī-gaṇa received an endowment of a tank for the same purposes in the 10th century.[3] Thus, they served as a means of rendering relief to the poor during the period under review.

1. *BKI*, iv; no. 4, p. 3.
2. Ibid. nos 6-7, pp. 6-7.
3 Ibid. i, pt. i, no 38, p. 23

CHAPTER VI

CONCLUSION

The Digambara monks, who advocated pristine purity and complete adherence to the canonical rules, came to stabilize their position in Karnataka by the beginning of the Christian era. They gradually became the most important sect and maintained their dominance in the field of religion and philosophy, literature, art and architecture from the 5th to the middle of the 12th century.

The most important change which affected the Jainas in Karnataka related to the way of their living. The wandering mode of life, originally intended for the monk community, yielded place to permanent habitation of the Jaina monks in Jaina monasteries. The Digambara teachers of Karnataka induced the people to erect monasteries and temples and endow them with rich gifts for proper maintenance. The Jaina devotees showed equal zeal for building residences for the Jaina ascetics. Gradually, Jaina monasticism organised itself under the authoritative control of the chief preceptors, who were generally the recipients of gifts on behalf of the Jaina temples and monastic establishments.

In the new monasticism, the preceptors wielded much authority over the monks and nuns. As the latter were solely dependent upon the former for their subsistence, they had to be loyal towards the preceptors. The preceptors also commanded respect of the lay devotees of all classes. Pūjyapāda, Jinasena, Guṇabhadra, Somadeva, Ajitasena, Sudatta, Vardhamānadeva and Municandra were some of the prominent Jaina teachers who exerted profound influence upon the kings and princes of Mysore in their own times. They now tendered advice not only on spiritual matters but also on worldly affairs. They took active interest in the politics of Karnataka. This obviously meant a break with the past, when the monks led a solitary life in the old monasticism. In any case, old norms were being freely violated.

Free intercourse between the monks and the Jaina householders, and the excessive dependence of the former upon the latter for their sustenance gave prominence to the Jaina laity in the new monastic life. Emphasis on the performance of *proṣodhaupavāsa* or fasting on the eighth and the fourteenth days in each fortnight among the laymen, which was invariably observed in the Jaina temples, brought them closer to each other.

With the rapid increase in the numbers of Jaina establishments, the Jaina monastic movements gained momentum. Several sects and monastic orders arose among the Digambara monks. The Jaina Church was divided into various units such as Saṅgha, gaṇa, gaccha and anvaya. The most important Digambara sect to appear in the period was that of the Yāpanīyas, who laid stress on the popular aspects of the Jaina religion. Contrary to the view of the orthodox Digambaras, they advocated salvation for women. They also strongly supported the use of occult methods in Karnataka. Through this practice, the monk Arkakīrti is recorded to have removed the bad influence of Saturn from Vimalāditya in the 9th century. Occult practices were popularized by other sects also. Indranandi of the Draviḍa Saṅgha advocated the worship of Yakṣiṇīs or mother cult in Karnataka during the closing years of the 10th century.

The Yāpanīyas concentrated first in the area around Palāśika or modern Halsi in the Belgaum district during the 5th-6th centuries. From there they extended their influence to Aihoḷe in the Bijapur district in the 7th century. They also founded monastic establishments in the Tumkur district during the 10th century. In the 11th-12th centuries, the Yāpanīyas gained prominence in the districts of Dharwar, Kolhapur and Belgaum.

The history of Jainism, which flourished vigorously in Karnataka during the 5th-12th centuries, reveals two important facts regarding the extension of its social basis. From the 5th century till the 9th century, Jainism in Karnataka seems to have thrived mainly under the patronage of the rulers, their ministers, nobles and other high officials of the state. It is fully substantiated by the large number of the donative records of this period which refer to the generous endowments made by the aristocratic people. Thus, this nullifies the popular erroneous belief that Jainism has always been a religion of the mercantile classes because between the 5th and the 9th centuries at least in Karnataka Jainism owes its expansion to the support of the rulers and administrators. But from the 10th century onwards, we have evidence to show the gradual extension of its social basis especially among the merchants, who embraced Jainism as ardently as the rulers and administrators during the 10th-12th centuries.

The absence of the merchant followers of Jainism in Karnataka in the early period (5th-9th centuries) can possibly be explained by the decline of trade and commerce not only in Karnataka but in the whole of southern India and the subsequent decrease in the social and economic status of the merchants. Further the few merchants that existed found it difficult to follow the puritan practices of the Jainas in the early stages. Only when commerce revived from the latter half of the 10th century the commercial class came into prominence in Karnataka. It was easy for them to join Jainism because by this time Jainas became more lax in the observance of their monastic conduct and practices. At any rate the number of merchant donors was smaller in comparison with that of the kings and princes even in the later period.

The material basis of the Jaina monasteries in Karnataka was provided by the generous benefactions made by the princes and rich persons. The donors patronized the Jaina monks and monasteries by transferring villages and innumerable plots of land. The donees earned considerable income from their corn-fields and gardens. The donation of oil mills, houses and the custom duties constituted another important source of income for the Jaina monasteries in Karnataka. On account of their huge wealth in landed property, the Jaina monks emerged as a land owning class in Karnataka in the early medieval period.

Monasteries in Karnataka did not serve exclusively as residence of monks and nuns. They discharged several important functions for the benefit of the Jaina community. The Jaina teachers imparted religious education in monasteries for which lands and villages were registered as gifts. Many Jaina monasteries in Karnataka ran charity houses which distributed food among the Jaina ascetics and gave shelter to the homeless.

The monks living in monasteries seem to have abandoned the puritan principles of Jainism. The building of monasteries and temples and donation of land, village and other things gave rise to laxity in morals among the Jaina monks. The Jaina vow of non-possession was easily set aside. On the contrary, they amassed huge fortunes and probably led a life of ease and comfort in the monasteries.

Though the medieval texts repeat and reflect the old rules regarding begging and diet, in practice things were getting different. The monks became flexible and slack in dietary practices. By old standards of conduct and character, they did not deserve food and other gifts. Somadeva tried to save the situation by diverting the attention of the Jaina devotees from the worthiness of the monk to the virtues of making gifts.

On the other hand, certain monks and lay devotees led extremely hard life leading to death. The Jaina practice of *sallekhanā* or religious sacrifice through fasting became popular among the Jainas in Karnataka during the 8th century. It gradually increased during the subsequent centuries and attracted the attention of the Jaina householders. It was not a substitute for *satī*, as has been supposed by some scholars, but an independent Jaina ritual.

The Jaina rituals also underwent major changes. The initiation rite and the rules for its performance were radically altered. The early Jaina scriptures do not exclude anybody from initiation on the ground of birth; on the other hand they vehemently oppose the caste system. But śūdras were kept out from initiation during this period. The Jainas were now so much affected by the Hindu *varṇa* scheme that the exclusion of the śūdras from *upanayana* came to be reflected in the Jaina system of initiation.

The ban on Vedic ritualism was lifted and the dominance of the priest class was revived among the Jainas. The worship of the Jinas in the Jaina temples became a costly affair, and the Brāhmaṇas were welcomed by the Jainas as priests who presided over their sacred ceremonies.

As a corollary to all this development, Jaina atheism lost ground during the early medieval age. The Jainas became as theistic as the Hindus. The Jinas were invested with the divine power of creation and destruction. They were credited with the same attributes of divinity as characterized the Brāhmaṇical gods—Śiva, Viṣṇu, and Śaṅkara. The Jaina teachers also explained to their followers several strange incarnations of Ṛṣabhadeva, the founder of the Jaina religion. All this shows the changed character of Jainism in Karnataka.

Thus, although the Digambara teachers advocated high-sounding puritan principles, they did not practise these in actual life. The practical idea of advancing the Jaina faith in Karnataka was their guiding force. They found it necessary to adjust themselves to the prevailing conditions. They therefore accepted some practices of the Hindus both in lay and monastic life. Probably this explains their survival in Mysore.

BIBLIOGRAPHY

I. Original Literary Sources

Āśādhara	*Jinasahasranāma*, Bhāratīya Jñānapiṭha Kāśī, 1954.
Amitagati	*Amitagati's Śrāvakācāra*, Paṇḍit Bhagcandra, Bombay, 1923.
—	*Yogasāra*, ed. Gajadharlal Nyāyatīrtha, Sanātana Jaina Granthmālā—16, Calcutta, 1918.
Amṛtacandra	*Puruṣārthasiddhyupāya*, Rāyacandra Jaina Śāstramālā—1, Bombay, 1904.
Cakravartī, Nemicandra Siddhānta	*Dravya Saṅgraha*, (ed.), S.C. Ghoshal, *SBJ*, vol. 1, The Central Jaina Publishing House, Arrah, 1917.
—	*Gommaṭasāra-Karma-Kāṇḍa*, SBJ, vol. VI, Pt.I, (ed.), J.L. Jaini, Lucknow, 1927.
Cāmuṇḍarāya	*Caitrasāra*, Māṇikcandra Digambara Jaina Granthkāryālaya—9, Bombay, 1917.
Devasena	*Darśanasāra*, (ed.), Nathu Ram Premi, Jaina Granthkāryālaya, Bombay.
Guṇabhadra	*Ātmānuśāsana*, (ed.) A. N. Upadhye and Hira lal Jain, Sholapur, 1961.
—	*Uttarapurāṇa*, (ed.), Pannalal Jain, Bhāratīya Jñānapīṭha, Kāśī, 1954.
Hariṣeṇa	*Bṛhatkathākosa*, (ed.), A.N. Upadhye, Bombay, 1943.
Indranandi	*Jvālinī-Kalpa*, An unpublished text, Hand-written manuscript, preserved in the Deva-kumar Oriental Jaina Library, Arrah, (Bihar).

Jaṭāsiṁhanandi *Varāṅgacarita*, (ed.). A.N. Upadhye, Māṇikcandra Digambara Jaina Granthmālā-40, Bombay, 1938.

Jinasena *Ādipurāṇa*, pt.I, with Hindi translation of the Sanskrit text, (ed.), Pannalal Jain, Second edition, Bhāratīya Jñānapīṭha, Kāśī, 1963.

— *Ādipurāṇa*, Pt. II, (ed.), Pannalal Jain, 1st edition, Bhāratīya Jñānapīṭha, Kāśī, 1951.

— *Pārśvābhyudaya* (ed.), M.G. Kothari, Bombay, 1965.

Kundakundācārya *Pravacanasāra*(ed.), A. N. Upadhye, Second edition, Bombay, 1935.

Mahāvīrācārya *Gaṇitasāra-Saṅgraha*, (ed.), L.C. Jain, Sholapur, 1963.

Malliṣeṇa Sūri *The Bhairava-Padmāvatī-kalpa*, (ed.), A. B. Abhyankar, Ahmedabad.

Mānatuṅga *Ādinātha-Stotra*, (ed.) Nathu Ram Premi, Bombay, 1916.

Pampa *Ādipurāṇa*, (ed.), K.G. Kundangar and A.P. Chauguler, Belgaum, 1953.

— *Vikramārjunavijaya*,(ed.), Venkatanarayanappa Belleve, Karnataka Sāhitya Pariṣad, Banglore, 1931.

Pūjyapāda *Sarvārthasiddhi*, (ed.), Phool Candra Siddhanta Sastri, Bhāratīya Jñānapīṭha Kāśī, 1st ed., 1955.

— *Pūjyapāda's Śrāvakācāra*, (ed.), Pannalal Wakalibal, Sholapur, 1933.

— *Samādhi-tantra*, (ed.), J.K. Mukhtar, Virasevamandir, Sarsawa, 1939.

Rāmacandra, Mumukṣu *Puṇyāsravakathākośa*, (ed.), A.N. Upadhye and H.L. Jain, Sholapur, 1964.

Ravisena *Padmapurāṇa*, Published with Hindi translation, vols. I-III, Bhāratīya Jñānapīṭha, Kāśī, 1958-59.

Śubhacandra *Jñānārṇava*, (ed.), Pannalal Wakalibal, Second edition, Bombay, 1913.

Sūri, Jinasena — *Harivaṁśapurāṇa*, vols. I-II, Māṇikcandra Digambara Jaina Granthmālā 32-33, Bombay.

Sūri, Somadeva — *Yaśastilaka*, Kāvyamālā 70-71, Nirṇayasāgara Press, Bombay, 1901-1903.

Sūri, Vādirāja — *Pārśvanāthacarita*, (ed.), Srilal Jain, Calcutta, 1922.

Umāsvāmī — *Tattvārthādhigama Sūtra*, vol. I, (ed.), J.L. Jaini, The Central Publishing House, Arrah, 1920.

Vasunandi — *Vasunandi Śrāvakācāra*, (tr.) H. L. Jain, Bhāratīya Jñānapīṭha, Kāśī, 1952.

Vaṭṭakera — Mūlācāra, pts. I-II, Māṇikcandra Digambara Jaina Granthamālā Samiti, Bombay, 1921-1923.

Vimala Sūri — *Paumacariya*, pt. I, (ed.), M. Santilal Vora, Varanasi, 1962.

Yogīndudeva — *Paramātmaprakāśa*, (ed.), A. N. Upadhye, Bombay, 1937.

— *Yogasāra*, (ed.), A.N. Upadhye, Bombay, 1937.

II. Archaeological Sources

Bombay Karnataka Inscriptions, vol. I, pt. I, (ed.), C.R. Krishnamacharlu and others, Madras, 1940.

Bombay Karnataka Inscriptions, Vol. IV, (ed.), G.S. Gai, Mysore, 1965.

Coorg Inscriptions, B.L. Rice, Revised edition, Madras, 1914.

Epigraphia Carnatica, vol. II, Inscriptions at Śravaṇa-Beḷgoḷa. R. Narasimhachar, Banglore, 1923.

Epigraphia Carnatica, vols. III-XII, Banglore, Manglore, 1898-1905.

Epigraphia Carnatica, vol. XIV, Supplementary Inscriptions in Mysore and Mandya districts, (ed.), M.H. Krishna, Mysore, 1943.

Epigraphia Carnatica, vol. XV, Supplementary Inscriptions in the Hassan district, (ed.), M.H. Krishna, Mysore, 1943.

Epigraphia Carnatica, vol. XVI, Supplementary Inscriptions in the Tumkur district, (ed.), K.A. Nilakanta Sastri, Mysore, 1958.

Epigraphia Carnatica, vol. XVII, Supplementary Inscriptions in the Kolar district, (ed.), M. Seshadri, Mysore, 1965.

Historical Inscriptions of Southern India, Robert Sewell, Madras, 1932.

Inscriptions published in Indian Antiquary, vols. VI-VIII, XII, XVIII-XIX, Bombay.

Karnataka Inscriptions, vol. I, (ed.), R.S. Panchamukhi, Dharwar, 1941.

Karnataka Inscriptions, vol. II, (ed.), R.S. Panchamukhi, Dharwar, 1952.

Mysore Archaeological Reports for the year 1910-1915, 1917, 1921, 1923, 1925-1927, 1932-1933, 1934-37, 1938-1945, Banglore.

South Indian Inscriptions, vol. IX, pt. I, (ed.), R. Shamsastri, Madras, 1939.

Topographical List of Inscriptions, vol. I-III, (ed.), V. Rangacharya, Madras, 1919.

III. Journals and Periodicals

Annals of the Bhandarkar Oriental Research Institute, Poona.

Anekānta, Hindi Journal, Delhi.

Bulletin of the Deccan College Post-graduate Research Institute, Poona.

Encyclopaedia of Religion and Ethics, ed. J. Hastings.

Indian Antiquary, Bombay.

Indian Culture, Calcutta.

Indian Historical Quarterly, Calcutta.

Jaina Antiquary, Arrah.

Jaina Siddhānta Bhāskara, Hindi Journal, Arrah.

Journal of Bihar and Orissa Research Society, Patna.

Journal of the Bombay Branch of the Royal Asiatic Society, Bombay.

Journal of the Bombay University, Bombay.

Journal of the Karnataka University, Dharwar.

New Indian Antiquary, Bombay.

Proceedings of the Indian History Congress.

Proceedings and Transactions of All India Oriental Conference.

The Quarterly Journal of the Mythic Society, Banglore.

IV. Secondary Works

Aiyanger, S. K. : *Ancient India and South Indian History and Culture*, vols. I-II, Poona, 1941.

Aiyer, K.V. Subrahmanya : *Historical Sketches of Ancient Dekkan*, vol. III, Coimbtore, 1969.

Altekar, A.S. : *The Rāṣṭrakūṭas and their Times*, Poona, 1934.

Appadorai, A. : *Economic Conditions in Southern India*, Madras, 1934.

Barua, B.M. : *Inscriptions of Aśoka*, pt. II. Calcutta, 1943.

Basham, A. L. : *History and Doctrines of the Ājivikas*, London, 1951.

Bhandarkar, R.G. : *Early History of the Dekkan*, Third edition, Calcutta, 1928.

Bhattacharya, B.C. : *Jaina Iconography*, Lahore, 1939.

Bhattacharya, H. : *The Jaina Prayer*, Calcutta, 1964.

Buhler, Johann Georg : *The Indian Sects of the Jainas* (tr.), Jas. Burgess, Second edition, Calcutta, 1963.

Burgess, Jas : *Digambara Jaina Iconography*, Reprinted from the Indian Antiquary vol. XXXII, 1903, Bombay, 1904.

Chakravarti, Chintaharan : *Tantras—Studies on their Religion and Literature*, 1st edition, Calcutta, 1963.

Chand, Bool : *Jainism in Indian History*, Varanasi, 1951.

Cousens, Henry : *The Cālukyan Architecures of the Kanarese districts*, Calcutta, 1926.

Deo S.B. : *History of Jaina Monachism from Inscriptions and Literature*, Poona,

— *Jaina Monastic Jurisprudence*, Banaras, 1960.

Deo, S.B. : *History of Jaina Monachism from inscriptions and literature*, Poona, 1956.

— : *Jaina Monastic Jurisprudence*, Benaras, 1960.

Desai, P.B. : *Jainism in South India and Some Jaina Epigraphs*, Sholapur, 1957.

Diwakar, R.R., ed. : *Karnataka Through the Ages*, Mysore, 1968.

Dutt, S.K. : *Buddhist Monks and Monasteries of India*, London, 1962.

Ehrenfels, Baron Omar Rolf, : *Mother Right in India*, Usmania University Series, Hyderabad, 1941.

Farquhar, J.N. : *An Outline of the Religious Literature of India*, First Indian reprint, Motilal Banarasidass, Delhi, 1967.

Fishcher, K.F. : *Caves and Temples of the Jainas*, Aliganj (U.P.), 1956.

Ganguly, O.C. : *The Art of the Rāṣṭrakūṭas*, Calcutta 1958.

Hukkerikerkar, R.S., (ed),: *Karnataka Darśana*, Bombay, 1955.

Handiqui, K.K. : *Yaśastilaka and Indian Culture*, Sholapur, 1949.

Herbert Stroup, : *Four Religions of Asia*, New York, 1968.

Iyer, L.K. Ananthakrishna and Others : *The Mysore Tribes and Castes*, vol. III, Mysore University, Mysore, 1930.

Jacobi, H. : *Jaina Sūtras*, pt. I, SBE, vol. XXII, Oxford, 1884.

— : *Jaina Sūtras*, pt. II, SBE, vol. XLV, Oxford, 1895.

— : *Studies in Jainism*, Ahmedabad, 1946.

Jain, Chhotelal : *Jaina Bibliography*, Calcutta, 1945.

Jain, C.R. : *The Practical Path*, The Central Jaina Publishing House, Arrah, 1917.

— : *The Household Dharma or the Ratnakaraṇḍa-Śrāvakācāra*, The Central Jaina Publishing House, Arrah, 1917.

Jain, J. P. : *Jaina Sources of the History of Ancient India*, Delhi, 1964.

Jaini, J.L. : *Outlines of Jainism*, Oxford, 1940.

Kalaghatagi, T.G. : *Some Problems in Jaina Psychology*, Dharwar, 1961.

Kane, P.V. : *History of Dharmaśāstra*, vol. II, pt. I, Bhandarkar Oriental Research Institute, Poona, 1941.

Karmakar, A.P. : *Cultural Heritage of Karnataka*, Dharwar, 1947.

Mazumdar, A.K. : *The Cālukyas of Gujarat*, Bombay, 1956.

Mazumdar, R.C. (ed.) : *The Classical Age*, Second impression, Bombay, 1962.

— : *The Age of Imperial Unity*, Third impression, Bombay, 1960.

— : *The Age of Imperial Kanauj*, First edition, Bombay, 1955.

Max Weber, : *The Religion of India : The Sociology of Hinduism and Buddhism*, Illinois, 1958.

Mehta, M.L. : *Jain Culture*, Varanasi, 1969.

Moraes, G.M. : *The Kadamba-kula*, Bombay, 1931.

Mugali, R.S. : *The Heritage of Karnataka*, Banglore, 1946.

Nandi, R.N. : *Religious Institutions and Cults in the Deccan*, Motilal Banarsidass, Delhi, 1973.

Radhakrishnan, S. : *Eastern Religions and Western Thought*, London, 1940.

Premi, N.R. : *Jaina Sāhitya aur Itihās*, Second edition, Bombay, 1956.

Radhakrishnan, S. : *Indian Philosophy*, vol. II, London, 1948.

Raghavan, V. : *Yantra or Mechanical Contrivances in Ancient India*, Bangalore, 1952.

Rao, M.V. Krishna : *The Gaṅgas of Talkad*, Madras, 1936.

Rice, E.P. : *A History of Kanarese Literature*, Second edition, London, 1921.

Rice, Lewis : *Mysore and Coorg from Inscriptions*, London, 1909.

Shah, C.J. : *Jainism in North India*, 800 B.C.—A.D. 526, London, 1932.

Sharma, R.S. : *Light on Early Indian Society and Economy*, Bombay, 1966.

Sharma, S.R. : *Jainism and Karnataka Culture*, Dharwar, 1940.

Shripal, Surendranath : *Colossus of Śravaṇa Beḷgoḷa and other Shrines of Deccan*, Bombay, 1953.

Saletore, B.A. : *Ancient Karnataka*, vol. I, History of Tuluva, Poona, 1936.

— : *Medieval Jainism*, Karnataka Publishing House, Bombay, 1938.

Schubring, Walther : *The Doctrines of the Jainas*, reprinted, Motilal Banarsidas, Delhi, 1962.

Sen, Amulachandra : *Schools and Sects of the Jaina Literature*, Calcutta, 1931.

Sitaramiah, V. : *Mahākavi Pampa*, Bombay, 1967.

Sastri, K.A. Nilakanta : *A History of South India*, Second edition, Oxford, 1958.

— : *Development of Religion in South India*, Madras, 1963.

— : *Sources of Indian History with special reference to South India*, Asia Publishing House, 1961.

Sastri S. Srikantha : *Sources of Karnataka History*, Mysore, 1940.

Stevenson, Mrs. Sinclair : *The Heart of Jainism*, Oxford, 1915.

Thurston, E., : *Castes and Tribes of Southern India*, vol. ii, Madras, 1909.

Venkataramanayya, N. : *The Cālukyas of Vemulavāḍa*, Hyderabad, 1953.

Warder, A.K. : *Outline of Indian Philosophy*, Delhi, 1971.

Williams, Robert : *Jaina Yoga*, London, 1963.

Winternitz, M. : *A History of Indian Literature*, vol. II, Calcutta, 1933.

Yazdani, G. : *The Early History of the Deccan* (pts. I-VI), London, 1960.

Dictionaries and Gazetteers

Apte, V.S. : *Sanskrit Hindi Kośa*, Motilal Banarsidass, 1966.

Kittel, Rev. F. : *Kannaḍa English Dictionary*, Oxford, 1894.

Monier Williams, M. : *A Sanskrit English Dictionary*, Oxford, 1951.

Mysore Gazetteer, vols. I-II, IV, New edition, (ed.), C. Hayavadana, Banglore.

APPENDIX—A

Districtwise arranged list of the donative records which register grants of land and village for the Jaina monks and monasteries during the 5th-12th centuries in Karnataka.

Sl. No.	*Name and findspots of Inscriptions*	*Date* A.D.	*Reference Book*
1.	Aihoḷe inscription of Pulakeśin II found on the east side of Meguṭi temple.	634	*EI*, vi, no. 1, pp. 11-2.
2.	Another record of the Rāṣṭrakūṭa king Kṛṣṇa II found at Aihoḷe.	911-2	*IA*, xii, p. 222.
3.	Arasibīḍi record of the Cālukya princess Akkādevī.	1047	*EI*, xvii, no. 10, pp. 121-3; BKI, i, pt. i, no. 103, pp. 99-100.
4.	Hoṇwād stone inscription of Someśvara I	1050	*IA*, xix, pp. 268-75.
5.	Hungund epigraph of Someśvara II.	1074	BKI, i, pt. i, no. 113.
	Belgaum District		
6.	Halsi copper plates of the Kadamba kings, seven in number, found in a small well called Cakratīrtha, at short distance outside Halsi in the Bīḍi taluq.	5th-6th centuries.	*IA*, vi, nos. 20-6.
7.	Gokak Plates of Dejja Mahārāja.	undated	*Ibid.* xxi, pp. 291ff.
8.	Four records of the Raṭṭa Chiefs namely Pṛithvirāma, Śāntivarmā, Aṅka and Lakṣmīdeva II found at Saundatti.	940 980 1048 1228	*JBBRAS*, x, pp. 194ff. *Ibid.* x, pp. 204ff. *Ibid.* pp., 172ff. *Ibid.* pp. 260ff.

9.	Huli record of Someśvara I found in the Vīrabhadra temple at Huli.	1043	*EI*, xviii, pp. 172ff.
10.	Koṇṇur record of the Raṭṭa chief Sena II.	1087	*JBBRAS*, x, pp. 287ff.
11.	The Nemīśvara *basadi* record found in Eksambi in Belgaun district.	1165	*MAR*, 1916, pp. 48-9.
	Kolhapur District		
12.	Altem copper plates of Pulakeśin I	489	*IA*, vii, no. xliv, pp. 209-15.
13.	Hoṇṇur record of the Śilahāra princes	Undated but assigned to 1110	*Ibid.* xii, p. 102 cited in P. B. Desai, op. cit, p. 119.
	Dharwar district		
14.	Devagiri copper plates of the Kadamba kings, three in number found in the bed of a tank at Devagiri.	5th-6th centuries.	*Ibid.* vii, nos. 35-7, pp. 34-8.
15.	Five records of the early Cālukya kings found on the slab of the Śaṅkha *basadi* at Lakshmeśvara in Shirhatti taluq.	683; 723; 730; 735; and one undated.	*BKI*, iv, nos. 3-7 pp. 3-7.
16.	Āḍūr stone inscription of the western Cālukya king Kīrtivarma II.	Undated but assigned to 750	*KI*, i, no. 3, pp. 4-5. *BKI*, iv, no. 9, p. 9.
17.	Aṇṇigere record of the Cālukya king Kīrtivarman II.	751-2	*Ibid*, i, pt. 1, no. 5, p. 3; *EI*, xxi, no. 34, p. 205.
18.	Koṇṇur inscription of the Rāṣṭrakūṭa king Amoghavarṣa.	860	*Ibid*, vi, no. 4, pp. 25-38.

19.	Bentūr record of the same king.	864	*BKI*, i, pt. 1, no. 10, p. 6.
20.	Mulgund record of Kṛṣṇa II.	902-3	*EI*, xiii, pp. 130ff.
21.	Venkaṭapur record of Amoghavarṣa.	906	*Ibid*. xvi, no. 4. pp. 59-62; *BKI*, i, pt. 1, no. 28, p. 16.
22.	Asuṇḍi record of Indra III.	925	*Ibid*, i, pt. 1, no. 34, p. 20.
23.	Kavajjgeri record of Govinda IV.	933	*Ibid*. no. 35, p. 21.
24.	Suddi copper plates of the Gaṅga king Būtuga.	938	*EI*, iii, no. 25, pp. 158ff.
25.	Naregel record of the Rāṣṭrakūṭa king Kṛṣṇa III.	950	*BKI*, i, pt. 1, no. 38, p. 23.
26.	Lakkuṇḍi record of Attimabbe	1007	*Ibid*. no. 52, p. 39.
27.	Hosur record of Jagadekamalla I.	1029	*Ibid*. no. 65, p. 55.
28.	Mugad epigraph of Someśvara I.	1045	*Ibid*. no. 78, p. 68.
29.	Mulgund record of the same later western Cālukya king.	1053	*EI*, xvi, pp. 53ff.
30.	Jāvur record of Jayakīrtideva	1059	P.B. Desai, op. cit., p. 143.
31.	Soraṭūr record of Someśvara II.	1071	*BKI*, i, pt. 1, no. 111, p. 108.
32.	Guḍigere Jaina record	1076	*IA*, xviii, pp. 35ff.
33.	Doṇi epigraph of the Cālukya king Vikramāditya VI.	1097	P.B. Desai, op. cit., p. 144.

Śravaṇa-Beḷgoḷa donative records found on the Candragiri, the Vindhyagiri and the village in the Hassan district.

34.	Śravaṇa-Beḷgoḷa record of the Gaṅga king Śivamāra II found on the Candragiri hill.	810	*EC*, ii, SB 415, p. 81.

35.	The Kūge-Brahmadeva Pillar inscription.	974	*EC.* SB 59, pp. 12-4.
36.	Three Śravaṇa-Beḷgoḷa epigraphs of Cāmuṇḍarāya and his son Jinadevana	982 983 995	*Ibid.* SB 121-2, pp. *Ibid.* SB 175-6, p. 89.
37.	Śravaṇa-Beḷgoḷa record of the Hoysaḷa general Gaṅga-Rāja found near the Śāsana *basadi.*	1117	*Ibid*, ii, SB 74, p. 40.
38.	Terina *basadi* record of Poysala seṭṭi.	1117	*Ibid.* SB 137, p. 64.
39.	Kattale *basadi* record of Gaṅga-Rāja.	1118	*Ibid.* SB 70, p. 37.
40.	Śāsana *basadi* record of the same general.	1118	*Ibid.* SB 73, pp. 38-40.
41.	Cāmuṇḍarāya *basadi* record of Pocikabbe, the mother of Gaṅga-Rāja.	1120	*Ibid.* SB 118, pp. 48-9.
42.	Another epigraph of Gaṅga-Rāja found near the Cāmuṇḍarāya *basadi.*	1123	*Ibid.* SB 117, pp. 47-8.
43.	Gandhavāraṇa *basadi* record of the Hoysaḷa queen Śāntaladevī.	1123	*Ibid.* SB 131, p. 58.
44.	Another record of the same queen found at the same place.	1123	*Ibid.* SB 132, pp. 58-60.
45.	Bāhubali Pillar inscription of the Hoysaḷa king Viṣṇuvardhana.	1131	*Ibid.* SB 143, pp. 70-5.
46.	Cāmuṇḍarāya *basadi* record of Bucana, son of Gaṅga-Rāja.	1133	*Ibid.* SB 120, p. 49.
47.	Śāntīśvara *basadi* record found at Jinanāthapura.	1135	*Ibid.* SB 384, pp. 165-7.
48.	Gommaṭeśvara records of	1159	*Ibid.* ii, SB 178, p 89.

No.	Record	Date	Reference
	the Hoysaḷa general Huḷḷa found on the Vindhyagiri hill.	1159	*EC*. SB 181, p. 89.
49.	Bhaṇḍāri *basadi* records of the same general.	1159 ,,	*Ibid*. SB 345 and 349, pp. 147-9; 151-4.
50.	Śravaṇa Beḷgoḷa epigraph of the same general.	1163	*Ibid*. SB 84, pp. 18-9.
51.	Gommaṭeśvara records of the Hoysaḷa general Huḷḷa and the Jewel merchants.	1175	*Ibid*. SB 240-1, pp. 101-3.
52.	Sāṇenahaḷḷi record of Gaṅga-Rāja.	1179	*Ibid*. SB 397, p. 169.
53.	Akkana *basadi* record of the Hoysaḷa king Vīra-Ballāla-deva.	1181	*Ibid*. SB 327, pp. 134-9.
54.	Siddhara *basadi* record of the same king and his councillor Candramaulī.	1181	*Ibid*. SB 256, p. 115.
55.	Gommaṭeśvara record of Basava-Seṭṭi.	1185	*Ibid*. SB 235, p. 101.
56.	Nagara-Jinālaya record of Vīra-Ballāla-deva and his minister Nāgadeva.	1195	*Ibid*. SB 335, pp. 132-4.
57.	Gommaṭeśvara record of Madukaṇṇa.	1196	*Ibid*. SB 237, p. 101.
58.	Gommaṭeśvara record of Someya-Seṭṭi.	1198	*Ibid*. SB 238, p. 101.

Mysore district

No.	Record	Date	Reference
59.	Kulagaṇa copper plates of the Gaṅga king Śivamāra II found in the village Kulagaṇa in the Chamrajanagar taluq.	Undated but assigned to the 7th-8th centuries.	*MAR*, 1925, p. 92.
60.	Devalapura record found at Devalapura in the Mysore taluq.	750	*EC*, iii, My 25, p. 3.

61.	Devarhaḷḷi copper plates found at Devarhaḷḷi in the Nagamangala taluq.	776	*EC* iv, Ng. 85, pp. 134-5.
62.	Vadaṇaguppe record of the Rāṣṭrakūṭa king Kambhādeva found at Devanur in the Nanjangud taluq.	808	*MAR*, 1927, p. 117.
63.	An undated record found in the village Hebbalguppe in the Heggaḍedevankote taluq.	825	*Ibid.* 1932, pp. 240-1.
64.	Tayalūr record found in the Mandya taluq.	895	*EC*, iii, Md. 13, p. 38.
65.	Keyatanhaḷḷi stone inscription found at Keyatanhaḷḷi in the Srirangapatna taluq.	900	*Ibid.* Sr. 147, p. 34.
66.	Rampura stone inscription found at Rampura in a paddy field in the Srirangapatna taluq.	904	*Ibid.* Sr. 148, p. 34.
67.	Kulagere stone inscription found at Kulagere in the Mallavalli taluq.	909	*Ibid.* iii, ML 30, p. 59.
68.	Būvanhaḷḷi Jaina record found on the pedestal of a Jaina image in the Candranātha *basadi* at Būvanhaḷḷi in the Hunsur taluq.	950	*MAR*, 1913, p. 31.
69.	Two Jaina epigraphs found at Cikka Hanasoge in the Yeḍatore taluq.	10th century.	*Ibid.* 1914, p. 38.
70.	Somasamudra record found in the village Somasamudra in the Mysore taluq.	993	*Ibid.* 1931, p. 139.
71.	Two more Jaina epigraphs found at Cikka Hanasoge in the Yeḍatore taluq.	1025	*EC*, iv, Yd. 21-2, p. 55.
72.	Another Cikka Haṇasoge record of the Yeḍatore taluq.	1080	*Ibid.* Yd. 23, p. 55.

73.	Still more another record found at the same place.	110	*EC.* Yd. 26, p. 56.
74.	The Pārśvanātha *basadi* record found in the Chamrajanagar taluq.	1117	*Ibid.* Ch. 83, p. 10.
75.	A record found at Basti Hosakote in the Krishnarajapete taluq.	1117	*MAR*, 1920, p. 32.
76.	Kambadahaḷḷi stone inscription found in the Nagamangala taluq.	1118	*EC*, iv, Ng. 19, p. 116.
77.	Sukadare stone inscription found in the same taluq.	1120	*Ibid.* Ng. 103, p. 141.
78.	Madeśvara temple stone inscription.	1164	*Ibid.* Ng. 30, p. 119.
79.	A record found at Kittur in the Heggadadevankote taluq.	1179	*MAR*, 1913, p. 37.
80.	Aḷesandra stone inscription found in the Nagamangala	1184	*EC*, iv, Ng. 32, pp. 120-2.
	Hassan district		
81.	Mararu stone inscription found at Mararu in the Arkalgud taluq.	900	*Ibid*, v, Ag. 24, p. 250.
82.	Belur inscription of the Gaṅga king Būtuga found at Belur.	952	*Ibid.* BL. 123, p. 80.
83.	Gubbi stone inscription found at Gubbi in the Hole-Narsipur taluq.	960	*Ibid.* HN14, p. 243.
84.	Goṇḍasi inscription found at Goṇḍasi in the Arsikere taluq.	970	*Ibid*, v, Ak. 164, p. 181.
85.	Manjarbad Jaina inscription found on the pedestal of a Jaina image.	970	*Ibid.* MJ. 67, p. 247.
86.	An epigraph found in the Somavara village in the Arkalgud taluq.	1060	*Ibid.* Ag. 98, p. 262.
87.	A damaged stone record found at Tolalu in the Belur taluq.	1060	*MAR*, 1927, pp. 43-4.

88. Another Somavara epigraph of the Koṅgāḷva king Adaṭarāditya.	1079	*EC*, V. Ag, 99, p. 263.
89. Hale-Beḷgoḷa record of the Hoysaḷa king Vinayāditya.	1094	*Ibid.* Cn. 148, pp. 189-90.
90. Śalya stone inscription of Viṣṇuvardhara.	1125	*Ibid.* Cn. 149, pp. 190-1.
91. Belur inscription of the same Hoysaḷa king.	1129	*MAR*, 1911, p. 43.
92. The Pārśvanātha *basadi* record found in the village Bastihaḷḷi in the Belur taluq.	1133	*EC*, V, BL. 124, pp. 81-4.
93. The Saumyanāyaki stone inscription of Viṣṇuvardhana found in the Belur taluq.	1136	*Ibid.* BL. 17, pp. 48-51.
94. The Muguli *basadi* stone inscription of Māri Seṭṭi and others.	1140	*Ibid.* Hn. 129, p. 36.
95. Another record of Viṣṇuvardhana found near the entrance of the Muguli *basadi.*	1147	*Ibid.* V, Hn. 130, pp. 36-7.
96. Heragu stone inscription of the Hoysaḷa king Narasiṁha-Deva.	1155	*Ibid.* Hn. 57, p. 16.
97. Karugunda stone record of the Hoysaḷa king Narasiṁhadeva.	1159	*Ibid.* Ak. 141, pp. 174-6.
98. Bandur stone inscription of the Hoysaḷa king Vīra-Ballāla-Deva.	1169	*Ibid.* Ak. 1, pp. 112-3.
99. Markuli stone record of the Hoysaḷa Ballāla-Deva.	1173	*Ibid.* Hn. 119, pp. 35-6.
100. Heragu epigraph of the Hoysala king Vīra-Ballāla-Deva.	1174	*Ibid.* Hn. 58, p. 17.
101. Bekka stone inscription.	1174	*Ibid.* Cn. 146, pp. 188-9.
102. Third Jaina epigraph found at Heragu in the Hassan taluq.	1176	*Ibid.* Hn. 59, p. 17.

103.	Bommenhaḷḷi stone record of the Hoysaḷa king Ballāla-Deva and his Councillor Candramaulī.	1182	*EC*, v, Cn. 150, pp. 192-3.
104.	Bastihaḷḷi record found near the entrance of the Pārśvanātha *basadi* in the Belur taluq.	1192	*Ibid.* BL. 129, pp. 86-7.
105.	Kumbenahaḷḷi stone inscription of Vīra-Ballāla-Deva.	1200	*Ibid.* V, Cn. 151, p. 193.
106.	Arasikere stone inscription of the same Hoysaḷa king and his Councillor Recharasa.	1220	*Ibid.* Ak. 77, pp. 140-1.
107.	Bastihaḷḷi record of the Hoysaḷa king Narasiṁga-Deva found in the Belur taluq.	1254	*Ibid.* BL. 125, p. 84.
108.	Another epigraph of the same king found at the same place.	1255	*Ibid.* BL. 126, p. 84.

Kadur district

109.	Siddagānahaḷḷi stone epigraph found in the Kadur taluq.	961	*Ibid.* vi, Kd. 159, p. 32.
110.	Kadur Pillar inscription	971	*Ibid.* Kd. 1, p. 1.
111.	Angadi stone inscription found at Angadi in the Mudgere taluq.	990	*Ibid.* Mg. 11, p. 60
112.	Another Angadi record of Vinayāditya Hoysaḷa.	1054	*Ibid.* Mg. 9, p. 60.
113.	Kaḍavanti stone inscription of Kandarpa Senamāra.	1060	*Ibid.* Cm. 75, pp. 43-4.
114.	Third Jaina record found at Angadi in the Mudgere taluq.	1063	*Ibid.* Mg. 13, p. 61.
115.	Mattavara epigraph of the Hoysaḷa king Vinayāditya and the merchant Māṇik Seṭṭi found in the Chikamagalur taluq.	1069	*MAR*, 1932, pp. 174-5.
116.	Brahmeśvara temple inscription of Siddhagiri of the Hoyasaḷa general Mariyane Daṇḍanāyaka.	1103	*EC*, VI, Cm. 169, pp. 56-7.

117.	Hantiyur record of Hariyabbarasi, daughter of Viṣṇuvardhana found on a ruined Jaina temple at Hantiyur in the Mudgere taḷuq.	1130	*EC*, vi, Mg. 22, pp. 62-3.
118.	Another Brahmeśvara temple record of the Hoysaḷa general Bharata found at Sindhagiri.	1137	*Ibid.* Cm. 161, 161, p. 58.
119.	A damaged stone inscription found at Kalasapura in the Kadur district.	1176	*MAR*, 1923, pp. 39-40.
	Shimoga district		
120.	The Guḍḍada *basadi* inscription of Tolapuruṣa Vikram Śāntara found in the Nagar taluq.	897-8	*EC*, viii, Nr. 60, pp. 154.
121.	Bandaṇike stone inscription found in the Shikarpur taluq.	902	*MAR*, 1911, p. 38.
122.	Kumśi stone inscription of Jinadatta-Rāya found in the Shimoga taluq.	950	*EC*, vii, Sk. 114, P. 37.
123.	Humcca stone inscription found at Humcca in the Nagar taluq.	958	*Ibid.* viii, Nr. 45, p. 146.
124.	Another Humcca epigraph of Bhujbala Śāntara found on the outerwall of Candraprabha *basadi* at Humcca.	1065	*Ibid.* Nr. 59, p. 154.
125.	Third Humcca record of Bhujbala Sāntara alias Trailokyamalla Deva found in the Nagar taluq.	1066	*Ibid.* Nr. 35, p. 137.
126.	The Śāntinātha *basadi* record of the Western Cālukya king Someśvara II found at Balligāme in the Shikarpur taluq.	1068	*Ibid.* vii, Sk. 136, pp. 102-4.
127.	Another Bandaṇike stone inscription of Someśvara II found at Bandaṇike in the Shikarpur talaq.	1075	*Ibid.* Sk. 221, p. 131.
128.	Baḍagiyara Hoṇḍa stone inscri-	1077	*Ibid.* vii, Sk.

	ption of Vikramāditya II and his general Brammadeva found at Shikarpur taluq.		124, pp. 95-6.
129.	Kuppaṭūr record found on the Pārśvanātha *basadi* in the Sorab taluq.	1077	*Ibid.* viii, Sb. 262, pp. 41-2.
130.	Fourth Humcca epigraph of the Śāntara lady Cāttaladevī found at Humcca in the Nagartaluq.	1077	*Ibid.* Nr. 35, pp. 137-8.
131.	Shikarpur epigraph of Bīneya Bammu Seṭṭi.	1080	*Ibid.* vii, Sk. 8, p. 39.
132.	Fifth Humcca record of Vikrama Śāntara.	1087	*Ibid.* viii, Nr. 40, p. 144.
133.	Bannikere record of Gaṅga Mahādevī found in the Shimoga district.	1115	*Ibid.* Sh. 97, p. 35.
134.	Kallūrguḍḍa stone record found near the Siddheśvara temple in Shimoga district.	1122	*Ibid.* Sh. 4, pp. 4-9.
135.	The stone inscription found in the old Jaina *basadi* at Chikka-magudi in the Shikarpur taluq.	1182	*Ibid.* vii, Sk. 197, p. 125.
136.	Uddhare epigraph of the Hoy-saḷa king Vīra-Ballāla-Deva and his minister Mahādeva found in the Sorab taluq.	1198	*Ibid.* viii, Sb. 140. p. 20.

Banglore district

137.	Hosakoṭe plates of the Gaṅga king Avinīta found at Hosakoṭe.	567	*MAR*, 1938, p. 86.
138.	Tolalu epigraph found at Tolalu found near the ruined Jaina *basadi*.	Undated	*Ibid.* 1926, p. 42.
139.	Maṇṇe copper-plates found at Maṇṇe in the Nelamangala taluq.	797	*EC*, ix, NL. 60, pp. 39-42.
140.	Bevuru stone inscription found in the Channapatna taluq.	900	*Ibid.* Cp. 69, p. 145.

141.	Another Maṇṇe epigraph of the Rāṣṭrakūṭa king Govinda III found in the Nelamangala taluq.	902	*EC*, ix, NL. 61, pp. 44-5.
	Kolar district		
142.	Noṇamangala copper plates found in the ruined Jaina *basadi* at Noṇamangla in the Malur taluq.	370	*Ibid.* x, ML. 73, p. 173.
143.	Another inscription found at Noṇamangala in the Malur taluq.	425	*Ibid.* ML. 72, p. 172.
144.	Narasāpur copper plates found at Narasāpur in the Kolar taluq.	903	*Ibid.* KL. 90, pp. 27-8.
	Chitaldroog district		
145.	Koramanga copper plates of Ravivarmā found at Koramanga in the Davangere taluq.	530	*MAR*, 1933, pp. 113-4.
146.	Bevinahaḷḷi stone inscription found in the Chitaldroog taluq.	968	*EC*, xi, Cd. 74, p. 16.
147.	Kuraḍi pillar inscription found at Kuraḍi in the Davangere taluq.	1060	*Ibid.* Dg., 140, p. 77.
148.	Sembanūr stone inscription found at Sembanūr in the Devangere taluq.	1062	*Ibid.* Dg. 143, pp. 77-8.
149.	The Śāntinātha *basadi* record of Holakere found in the Chitaldroog district.	1154	*Ibid.* Hk. 1, p. 115.
	Tumkur district		
150.	Kadaba copper plates found at Kadaba in the Gubi taluq.	812	*Ibid.* xii, Gb. 61, pp. 30-1.
151.	Biḍare stone inscription found at Biḍare in the Gubi taluq.	979	*Ibid.* Gb. 57, p. 27.
152.	Hemāvatī stone inscription found in the Sira taluq.	982	*Ibid.* Si. 27, p. 92.
153.	Candraśāle *basadi* record of Haṭana found at Hatana in the Tiptur taluq.	1078	*Ibid.* xii, Tp. 101, pp. 61-2.

154.	Kaidāla stone epigraph of the Hoysaḷa king and his minister Guli-Bāci found in the Tumkur taluq.	1151	*EC*, xii, Tm.8, pp. 3-4.
155.	Paṇḍitarahaḷḷi stone inscription found in the Tumkur taluq.	1160	*Ibid.* Tm. 38, p 10.
156.	Haggare stone epigraph found in the Chiknayakanhaḷḷi taluq.	1160	*Ibid.* Ck. 21, pp. 77-8.
157.	Karaḍālu Pillar inscription found in the Tiptur taluq.	1174	*Ibid.* Tp. 53, p. 60.
158.	Yādagatta stone record of Vīra-Ballāla-Deva found in the Chiknayakanhaḷḷi taluq.	1188	*Ibid.* Ck 20, p. 76.

Coorg district

159.	Mercāra copper plates of the Gaṅga king Avinīta found at Mercāra in the Coorg district.	466	*Ibid.* i, Cg. 1, pp. 51-2.
160.	Biliyūr stone inscription of Rācamalla II.	888	*Ibid.* Cg. 2, pp. 52-3.
161.	Peggūr stone inscription	978	*Ibid.* Cg. 4, p. 53.
162.	Two stone inscriptions found at Nallūr.	1050	*Ibid.* i, Cg. 30-1, pp. 64-5.
163.	Mullūr stone records	1050	*Ibid.* Cg. 37-8, p. 66.

Cuddapah district

164.	Dānavulapāḍu stone inscription found in the village Dānavulapāḍu.	Undated	*SII*, ix, pt. 1, p. 36.
165.	Another record of Śrīvijaya found at Dānavulapāḍu	Undated but assigned to the 10th-11th centuries.	*EI*, x, pp. 147-53.

Raichur district

166.	Uppina-Betagiri stone inscription found near the village Uppina-Betagiri fifteen miles from Kopbal.	964	P.B. Desai, op. cit., pp. 367-9.
167.	Another record found at Kopbal.	10th century.	P.B. Desai, op. cit., pp. 343-4.

APPENDIX—B

Numerical strength of deaths of monks, nuns and lay devotees by the Jaina vow of *Sallekhanā* during the 7th-12th centuries.

S.N.	*Name of the Sacrificer*	*Date*	*Place*	*Books of Reference*
1.	Prabhācandra	600	Cikka-beṭṭa or Candragiri hill at Śravaṇa-Beḷgoḷa.	*EC*, ii, SBI, p. 1.
2.	Kanakasena and Baladeva Muni	650	,,	*Ibid.* SB 2, p. 2.
3.	Ariṣṭanemi	,,	,,	*Ibid.* SB 11, p. 4.
4.	Śāntisena	,,	,,	*Ibid.* SB 31, p. 7.
5.	Vṛsabhanandi	,,	,,	*Ibid.* SB 75, p. 40.
6.	Tīrthada-goravaḍigal	700	,,	*Ibid.* SB 5, p. 3.
7.	Ullikal-goravaḍigal	,,	,,	*Ibid.* SB 6, p. 3.
8.	Guṇasena-Guruvar	,,	,,	*Ibid.* SB 8, p. 3.
9.	Panapa-bhaṭāra	,,	,,	*Ibid.* SB 9, p. 3.
10.	Caritraśrī	,,	,,	*Ibid.* SB 12, p. 4.
11.	Sarvajña-bhaṭāra	,,	,,	*Ibid.* SB 13, p. 4.
12.	Unnamed monk	,,	,,	*Ibid.* SB 17, p. 5.
13.	Unnamed monk	,,	,,	*Ibid.* ii, SB 19, p. 5.
14.	Akṣakīrti	,,	,,	*Ibid.* SB 21, p. 5.
15.	Kalantūr	,,	,,	*Ibid.* SB 22, pp. 5-6.
16.	Guṇadeva	,,	,,	*Ibid.* SB 23, p. 6.
17.	Baladeva-Goravaḍigal	,,	,,	*Ibid.* SB 24, p. 6.
18.	Ugrasena Goravaḍigal	,,	,,	*Ibid.* SB 25, p. 6.
19.	Unnamed monk	,,	,,	*Ibid.* SB 26, p. 6.
20.	Māsena	,,	,,	*Ibid.* SB 27, pp. 6-7.

21. Mellagavāsa-Guruvar	700	Cikka-betṭa or Candragiri hill.	*EC*, ii, SB 28, p. 7.
22. Guṇabhūṣita	,,	,,	*Ibid*. SB 29, p. 7.
23. Unnamed teacher	,,	,,	*Ibid*. SB 30, p. 7.
24. Siṅganandi	,,	,,	*Ibid*. SB 32, p. 7.
25. Unnamed monk	,,	,,	*Ibid*. SB 33, p. 7.
26. Nāgasena-Goravaḍigal	,,	,,	*Ibid*. SB 34, p. 8.
27. Sarvanandi	750	,,	*Ibid*. SB 36, p. 8.
28. Unnamed Monk	700	,,	*Ibid*. ii, SB 77, p. 41.
29. Śaucācārya	750	,,	*Ibid*. SB 79, p. 41.
30. Mahādeva	700	,,	*Ibid*. SB 80, p. 41.
31. Īśāna-Parmeṣṭhi	,,	,,	*Ibid*. SB 81, p. 41.
32. Baladevācārya	,,	,,	*Ibid*. SB 82, p. 42.
33. Candradevācārya	,,	,,	*Ibid*. SB 84, p. 42.
34. Puṣpanandi	750	,,	*Ibid*. SB 85, p. 42.
35. Nandisena	700	,,	*Ibid*. SB 88, p. 42.
36. Viśoka-bhaṭāra	,,	,,	*Ibid*. SB 92, p. 43.
37. Unnamed monk	,,	,,	*Ibid*. SB 93, p. 43.
38. Indranandī-ācārya	,,	,,	*Ibid*. SB. 95, p. 43.
39. Unnamed monk	,,	,,	*Ibid*. SB 96, p. 43.
40. Śrī-ācārya	,,	,,	*Ibid*. SB 102, p. 44.
41. Puṣpasenācārya	,,	,,	*Ibid*. SB 103, p. 44.
42. Śrīdevācārya	,,	,,	*Ibid*. SB 104, p. 44.
43. Guṇakīrti	,,	,,	*Ibid*. SB 105, p, 44.
44. Vṛṣabhanandi	,,	,,	*Ibid*. ii, 106, p. 44.
45. Meghanandi	,,	,,	*Ibid*. SB 109, p. 45.
46. Nandimuni	,,	,,	*Ibid*. SB 111, p. 45.
47. Devasena	,,	,,	*Ibid*. SB 113, p. 45.
48. Puritiya	,,	,,	*Ibid*. SB 115, p. 46.
49. Ariṣṭanemideva	800	,,	*Ibid*. SB 14, p. 4.
50. Mahāvīra	,,	,,	*Ibid*. SB 15, p.4.
51. Kami-bhaṭāra	900	,,	*Ibid*. SB 62, p. 14.
Name of the nuns			
52. Dhaṇṇekuṭṭarvī	700	,,	*Ibid*. SB 7, p. 3.
53. Jambu-nāyagir	,,	,,	*Ibid*. SB 18, p. 5.
54. Nāgamatī-gantiyar	,,	,,	*Ibid*. SB 20, p. 5.

No.	Name	Date	Place	Reference
55.	Śasīmatī-ganti	700	Cikka-beṭṭa or Candragiri hill at Śravaṇa Beḷgoḷa	*EC*, ii, SB 76, p. 41.
56.	Rājñīmatī-ganti	,,	,,	*Ibid.* SB 97, p. 43.
57.	Anantāmatī-gan	,,	,,	*Ibid.* SB 98, p. 43.
58.	Māvī-abbe	,,	,,	*Ibid.* SB 107, p. 45.
59.	Āryā	,,	,,	*Ibid.* SB 108, p. 45.
60.	Guṇamatī-avve	,,	,,	*Ibid.* SB 112, p. 45.
61.	Prabhāvatī and Damitāmatī	,,	,,	*Ibid.* SB 114, pp. 45-6.
62.	Meghacandratraividya	1115	,,	*Ibid.* SB 126, p. 55.
63.	Śrīmatī-ganti	1119	,,	*Ibid.* SB. 156, p. 77
64.	Śubhacandra-Siddhāntadeva	1120	,,	*Ibid.* SB 117, pp. 47-8.
65.	Hoysaḷa Seṭṭi	1120	,,	*Ibid.* SB 159, p. 78.
66.	Mācikabbe	1131	,,	*Ibid.* SB 123, p. 73.
67.	Baladeva	1139	,,	*Ibid.* SB 141, p. 68.
68.	Singimayya	1139	,,	*Ibid.* SB 142, p. 70.
69.	Prabhācandra Siddhāntadeva	1145	,,	*Ibid.* SB 140, p. 67.
70.	Devakīrti	1165	,,	*Ibid.* SB 63, p. 16
71.	Sarvanandi	881	At Kopbal in the Raichur district	B.A. Saletore, op, cit., p. 193.
72	Candrasenācārya	900	At Bevuru in the Banglore dist.	*EC*, ix, Cp. 69, p. 145.
73.	Nāgasena	900	,,	*Ibid.* Cp. 70, p. 145.
74.	Nemicandra	900	Cikka Hanasoge in the Yeḍatore taluq.	*MAR*, 1914, p. 38.
75.	Elācārya	910	,,	*Ibid.* 1914, p. 38.
76.	Trilokacandra-bhaṭāra	979	At Biḍare in the Tumkur district.	*EC*, xii, Gb. 57, p. 27.
77.	Unnamed monk	980	At the village Barun in the Mysore district.	*Ibid.* iii. My 40, p. 4.
78.	Vimalacandra-paṇḍita	990	At Angadi in the Kadur district.	*Ibid.* VI, 11, Mg. 11, p. 60.

79. Mahendrakīrti century	10th	Cikka-Hanasage in the Yoḍatore taluq.	*MAR*, 1913, p. 31.
80. Vajrapaṇḍita	1040	At Angadi in the Kadur district.	*EC*, vi, Mg. 17, p. 61.
81. Kiviriyya	1050	At Nallūru in the Coorg district.	*Ibid.* 1, Cg. 30, p. 64.
82. Jakkiyabbe	1050	At Nallūru in Coorg district.	*Ibid.* Cg. 31, pp. 64-5
83. Guṇasena	1064	At Mullūru in the the coorg district.	*Ibid.* Cg. 34, p. 65
84. Boppave	1090	At Tīrthahalli in the Shimoga dist.	*Ibid.* VIII, TL. 198, p. 207.
85. Vādībhasiṁha	1090	At Bale-Honnūr in the Kepa taluq.	*Ibid.* VI, Kp. 3, p. 75
86. Maladhārideva	1093	At Tīrthahaḷḷi	*Ibid.* VIII, TL. 199, p. 207.
87. Vardhamānadeva	10th	Century at Sāgarkaṭṭe	*MAR*, 1929, p. 109.
88. Ge-ganti	1120	At Chikmagalur in the Kadur dist.	*EC*, VI, Cm 52, p. 40.
89. Bīrayya	1120	At Yeḍatore	*Ibid.* IV, Yd. 50, p. 59.
90. Meghacandrabhaṭṭāraka	1163	At Chiknayakan haḷḷi in the Tumkur district.	*Ibid.* XII. CK. 23. p. 78.
97. Ajitasenadeva	1170	At Manjarabad in the Hassan district.	*Ibid.* V, Mj. 133, pp. 108-9.
92. Haryale	1174	At Tiptur in the Tumkur district.	*Ibid.* XII, TP. 93. p. 60.
93. Hariharadevī	1174		*Ibid.* Tr. 94, p. 61.
94. Śubhacandra	1213	At Bandalike in the shimoga dist.	*Ibid.* VII. Sk. 226, p.133.

INDEX

E

F

G

ERRATA

Page	*Line*	*For*	*Read*
2	7	Koppal	Kopbel
6	fn. 1	EC	EC,
8	fn. 2	Ibid	Ibid.
10	fn. 2	E P. Rice	E.P. Rice
13	22	Vemulvāda	Vemulvāḍa
14	fn. 4, 5	E P. Rice M Winternitz	E.P. Rice M. Winternitz
16	31	Umāsvāmi	Umāsvāmī
19	fn. 2	EC	EC,
20	fn. 2	EC.	EC,
24	fn. 3	A N. Upadhye	A.N. Upadhye
28	fn. 3	T.G. Kalaghatgi.	T.G. Kalaghat- gi,
30	fn. 3	Ibid.,	Ibid.
31	12	Ṛiṣabhadeva	Ṛṣabhadeva
35	fn. 5	Ibid,	Ibid.
39	fn. 3	EI.	EI,
43	fn. 6	Ibid,	Ibid.
53	18	Nilagiri	Nīlagiri
54	fn. 4, 5	Ibid,	Ibid.
61	fn. 3	Jaīn	Jain
64	fn. 1	EC.	EC,
95	fn. 2	Ibid	Ibid.
101	32	Kaveri	Kāverī
111	fn. 2	Ibid,	Ibid.
112	fn. 4	Ibid,	Ibid.
115	fn. 4	Ibid	Ibid.
131	fn. 4	SII.	SII,
132	fn. 3	IA.	IA,

ADDENDUM

Please read Baṅkāpur, Hariṣeṇa, Lakṣmeśvara and Raviṣeṇa without diacritical marks.